P9-CSU-641

THE RIGHT TO
A TRIAL BY JURY

Other books in this series:

THE RIGHT TO A TRIAL BY JURY

Edited by Robert Winters

Bruce Glassman, *Vice President*
Bonnie Szumski, *Publisher*
Helen Cothran, *Managing Editor*
Scott Barbour, *Series Editor*

GREENHAVEN PRESS
An imprint of Thomson Gale, a part of The Thomson Corporation

THOMSON
™
GALE

Detroit • New York • San Francisco • San Diego • New Haven, Conn.
Waterville, Maine • London • Munich

THOMSON
━━━━━✳━━━━━ ™
GALE

Coweta County Public Library System
85 Literary Lane
Newnan, GA 30265

© 2005 by Greenhaven Press, a part of The Thomson Corporation.

Thomson and Star Logo are trademarks and Gale and Greenhaven Press are registered trademarks used herein under license.

For more information, contact
Greenhaven Press
27500 Drake Rd.
Farmington Hills, MI 48331-3535
Or you can visit our Internet site at http://www.gale.com

ALL RIGHTS RESERVED.
No part of this work covered by the copyright hereon may be reproduced or used in any form or by any means—graphic, electronic, or mechanical, including photocopying, recording, taping, Web distribution or information storage retrieval systems—without the written permission of the publisher.

Every effort has been made to trace the owners of copyrighted material.

Cover credit: © Bettmann/CORBIS. Jurors listen to testimony in November 1954 during the murder trial of Dr. Samuel Sheppard.
Dover Publications, 92
Library of Congress, 15
National Archives, 51

LIBRARY OF CONGRESS CATALOGING-IN-PUBLICATION DATA

The right to a trial by jury / Robert Winters, book editor.
    p. cm. — (The Bill of Rights)
ISBN 0-7377-1937-0 (lib. : alk. paper)
    1. Jury—United States. 2. Jury—United States—History. I. Winters, Robert, 1963– . II. Bill of Rights (San Diego, Calif.)

KF8972.A5.R54 2005
345.73'056—dc22   2004052282

Printed in the United States of America

"I cannot agree with those who think of the Bill of Rights as an 18th Century straightjacket, unsuited for this age. . . . The evils it guards against are not only old, they are with us now, they exist today."

—Hugo Black, associate justice of the
U.S. Supreme Court, 1937–1971

The Bill of Rights codifies the freedoms most essential to American democracy. Freedom of speech, freedom of religion, the right to bear arms, the right to a trial by a jury of one's peers, the right to be free from cruel and unusual punishment—these are just a few of the liberties that the Founding Fathers thought it necessary to spell out in the first ten amendments to the U.S. Constitution.

While the document itself is quite short (consisting of fewer than five hundred words), and while the liberties it protects often seem straightforward, the Bill of Rights has been a source of debate ever since its creation. Throughout American history, the rights the document protects have been tested and reinterpreted. Again and again, individuals perceiving violations of their rights have sought redress in the courts. The courts in turn have struggled to decipher the original intent of the founders as well as the need to accommodate changing societal norms and values.

The ultimate responsibility for addressing these claims has fallen to the U.S. Supreme Court. As the highest court in the nation, it is the Supreme Court's role to interpret the Constitution. The Court has considered numerous cases in which people have accused government of impinging on their rights. In the process, the Court has established a body of case law and precedents that have, in a sense, defined the Bill of Rights. In doing so, the Court has often reversed itself and introduced new ideas and approaches that have altered the legal meaning of the rights contained in the Bill of Rights. As a general rule, the Court has erred on the side of caution, upholding and expanding the rights of individuals rather than restricting them.

An example of this trend is the definition of cruel and unusual punishment. The Eighth Amendment specifically states, "Excessive bail shall not be required, nor excessive fines imposed, nor cruel and unusual punishments inflicted." However, over the years the Court has had to grapple with defining what constitutes "cruel and unusual punishment." In colonial America, punishments for crimes included branding, the lopping off of ears, and whipping. Indeed, these punishments were considered lawful at the time the Bill of Rights was written. Obviously, none of these punishments are legal today. In order to justify outlawing certain types of punishment that are deemed repugnant by the majority of citizens, the Court has ruled that it must consider the prevailing opinion of the masses when making such decisions. In overturning the punishment of a man stripped of his citizenship, the Court stated in 1958 that it must rely on society's "evolving standards of decency" when determining what constitutes cruel and unusual punishment. Thus the definition of cruel and unusual is not frozen to include only the types of punishment that were illegal at the time of the framing of the Bill of Rights; specific modes of punishment can be rejected as society deems them unjust.

Another way that the Courts have interpreted the Bill of Rights to expand individual liberties is through the process of "incorporation." Prior to the passage of the Fourteenth Amendment, the Bill of Rights was thought to prevent only the federal government from infringing on the rights listed in the document. However, the Fourteenth Amendment, which was passed in the wake of the Civil War, includes the words, ". . . nor shall any state deprive any person of life, liberty, or property, without due process of law; nor deny to any person within its jurisdiction the equal protection of the laws." Citing this passage, the Court has ruled that many of the liberties contained in the Bill of Rights apply to state and local governments as well as the federal government. This process of incorporation laid the legal foundation for the civil rights movement—most specifically the 1954 *Brown v. Board of Education* ruling that put an end to legalized segregation.

As these examples reveal, the Bill of Rights is not static. It truly is a living document that is constantly being reinterpreted and redefined. The Bill of Rights series captures this vital aspect of one of America's most cherished founding texts. Each volume in the series focuses on one particular right protected in the Bill of Rights. Through the use of primary and secondary sources, the right's evolution is traced from colonial times to the present. Primary sources include landmark Supreme Court rulings, speeches by prominent experts, and editorials. Secondary sources include historical analyses, law journal articles, book excerpts, and magazine articles. Each book also includes several features to facilitate research, including a bibliography, an annotated table of contents, an annotated list of relevant Supreme Court cases, an introduction, and an index. These elements help to make the Bill of Rights series a fascinating and useful tool for examining the fundamental liberties of American democracy.

Juries constitute one of the last vestiges of direct democracy. As jurors, average Americans assume powers that other cultures have left in the hands of kings and lords or, at least, trained and carefully selected judges. Juries drawn from a cross-section of the populace decide on questions of guilt or innocence, freedom or imprisonment, massive fines in the form of punitive damages, even life or death. For most Americans it is hard to imagine a fair system of criminal justice without jury trials, but the truth is that most countries, including most democracies, have chosen to keep criminal justice in the hands of trained professionals or traditional elites. Partly by historical accident but also very much by design, the United States has retained this legacy from medieval England, and by this time most Americans simply take it for granted.

For the Founders, the jury was a matter of vital interest. In its list of complaints against George III, the Declaration of Independence condemned the king for "depriving us, in many cases, of the benefits of Trial by Jury." Article III of the Constitution guarantees jury trials in criminal cases, specifying that these trials will be held in the state in which the crime was committed. Not satisfied with this assurance, the Constitution's critics insisted that the right to a public trial by an impartial jury in both criminal and most civil cases be guaranteed. As a result the Sixth and Seventh amendments codify the right to a jury trial in criminal and civil cases, respectively. Citing jury trials three times in the Constitution could be viewed as overkill, considering that such fundamental rights as freedom of speech, religion, and the press fit neatly into the First Amendment. But for the revolutionary generation, the right to trial by jury was the final bulwark against arbitrary government, the linchpin that held these rights in place. As Thomas Jefferson put it in a letter to Tom Paine, "I consider [trial by jury] as the only anchor ever yet imagined by man, by which a government can be held to the principles of its constitution."

From King's Prerogative to People's Safeguard

While juries have their antecedents in the Athenian democracy (such as the jury that condemned Socrates to death) and some Viking customs, most scholars agree that the beginnings of the modern jury system can be traced to medieval England. Justice, so-called, in the early Middle Ages consisted largely of putting the accused to the "proof," which could be done in several ways. One method was "compurgation," in which the defendant and character witnesses swore to the defendant's innocence in a series of complicated oaths that had to be done exactly, or the "oath was burst" and the accused was found guilty. For more serious offenses, or less reputable defendants, the accused was subjected to an ordeal, which might mean being thrown into a pool or forced to hold a red-hot iron. Innocence was proved by sinking to the bottom of the pool (and hopefully a quick retrieval before drowning) or by having a clean wound three days after holding the iron. When the Normans conquered England in 1066 they brought with them the trial by battle, another form of ordeal, but they also brought a different kind of trial: the inquest.

While ordeals were generally overseen by priests or local lords, inquests were conducted by a representative of the crown, who would bring together a group of local knights and respectable freemen to settle disputes about taxes, land ownership, or misconduct. Unlike today's impartial juries, these men were chosen precisely because they were likely to know the facts and the reputation of the parties in any dispute. They were actually more like witnesses than jurors as they are known today; their role was to help the judge decide the facts. Generally, these inquests looked into civil matters, but under Henry II (1154–1189) they began to expand their reach into serious criminal matters, which the king saw as offenses against the entire realm.

While Henry II did not go so far as to abolish the older forms of trial, he instituted a system that prefigured contemporary grand juries. Under this system twelve knights or freemen would formally accuse a subject before he was put to the proof. At the same time, the inquest was used aggressively to defend the king's financial interests throughout the realm. New royal judges were sent on circuit around the country. Nineteeth-century legal scholar Sir James Fitzjames Stephen describes their role in securing the king's property and revenue: "The rigorous enforcement of all the proprietary and other profitable rights of the Crown . . . was naturally associated with their duties as administrators of the criminal law, in which the King was deeply interested, not only because it protected the life and property of his subjects, but also because it contributed to the revenues."

For centuries the juries remained largely under the control of judges appointed by the sovereign. The Magna Carta, which King John was forced to sign in 1215, does guarantee an appeal to juries, but was much more limited than the words imply today. When trial by ordeal or battle was abolished, juries took on a new importance, gradually becoming less like witnesses and more like the impartial judges of facts they are today. But the actual judges remained in charge. In addition to keeping juries without food or water until they reached a verdict, judges could send juries back to deliberation or even fine and imprison them for delivering the "wrong verdict."

The subservient role of juries finally began to change in 1670, when Quaker William Penn was dragged into court. Despite the judge's express instructions, the jury refused to convict Penn of unlawful assembly merely for giving a sermon about his beliefs. Five times the judge sent the jurors back to deliberate, and five times they returned with the same verdict. Finally, he imposed a fine and ordered the jurors to be held in prison until the fine was paid. When outraged jurors filed a writ of habeas corpus (which requires the government to formally charge the accused or else to free him), Chief Justice John Vaughn released them, establishing the jury's right to reach a verdict based on their own convictions.

A Right Embraced by Americans

William Penn went on to found Pennsylvania in a land where trial by jury would flourish even more than in England. All of the thirteen colonies included the right to jury trial in their founding charters. Colonists were even more jealous of this right than their English counterparts because of their greater suspicion of royal judges as well as the entire legal profession. The colonies had their own "Penn case" in 1735, when publisher John Peter Zenger was charged with seditious libel. Best known as the case that established freedom of the press as an American right, the case also cemented the right of juries to judge the law as well as the facts. Zenger was tried for seditious libel when his newspaper published articles that criticized a royal governor. At that time, the law stated that truth was not a defense for libel; that is, even if the statements were true, a publisher could be convicted for libel for publishing them. Despite the judge's express instructions that truth was not a defense against seditious libel of public officials, the jury found Zenger not guilty based on the defense attorney's argument that the "libels" were substantially true. While the old libel laws remained in place, prosecutors stopped bringing these kinds of cases to trial because they realized that juries would not convict if truth were a defense.

By the time of the Revolutionary War, juries were well established in the American mind as defenders of rights against the arbitrary power of governors and judges. The Continental Congress declared that colonists were entitled "to the great and inestimable privilege of being tried by their peers of the vicinage [locality]." The same spirit animated the opponents of the Constitution when it came time to decide on ratification. Anti-Federalists declared that the Constitution's express guarantee of the right to trial by jury in criminal cases was an underhanded attempt to eliminate the jury in civil cases. They feared that the government might eliminate juries altogether if it could figure out a way to turn criminal cases into civil cases. Eventually, of course, the Constitution was ratified, but the First Congress rushed to complete a bill of rights, including the right to trial by jury in both civil and criminal cases.

A Profoundly Democratic Institution

The American jury grew up in tandem with American democracy, gaining independence and assertiveness as the colonists

Women register for jury duty in 1937. Trial by jury is a fundamental American right that continues to be surrounded by controversy.

grew more restless and less subservient. By putting so much judicial power in the hands of ordinary jurors, the United States made a profound commitment to the basic principle of democracy: the power of the people. Democracy's blessings and curses have been on full display in jury trials. Northern juries once protected fugitive slaves from their masters. Southern juries once protected racist vigilantes from justice. The O.J. Simpson verdict sparked outrage and calls for abolishing the jury system. The Rodney King verdict sparked a bloody riot. At the same time, unpopular activists like Angela Davis and Father Philip Berrigan have found relief from jurors who refused to give in to government pressure or their own prejudices.

Perhaps nothing illustrates Americans' ambivalence toward jury powers so much as the controversial doctrine known as jury nullification—the right of juries to judge the law itself as well as the facts of the case. It was precisely this doctrine that allowed the jury to acquit Zenger in the face of the libel laws as written, and for much of American history this aspect of juries was generally affirmed. The renowned Supreme Court justice Oliver Wendell Holmes declared in

1920, "The jury has the power to bring a verdict in the teeth of both the law and the facts." At one time jurors were routinely informed of this right by the judge, but in 1895 the Supreme Court ruled that this right was no longer a requirement to ensure a just verdict. More recently, jury nullification has come under greater attack, and some who have tried to inform jurors of this power have been charged with jury tampering. Some are outraged by this situation; organizations and books are attempting to spread the word that juries can decide law as well as fact. Others are deeply concerned that unelected juries could essentially unmake laws passed by representative assemblies or substitute their own judgment for the express will of the majority of citizens. This controversy goes to the heart of Americans' feelings toward juries and the powers that have been put in their hands.

Other controversies will continue to surround this long-standing right. The nation will face questions about the propriety of jury trials, as opposed to military tribunals, in the ongoing war on terrorism. Jury verdicts will occasionally stun and outrage the public, and from time to time commentators will call for eliminating juries altogether (although this would require the unprecedented step of repealing two of the amendments in the Bill of Rights as well as part of Article III). Worries about jurors' competence to handle complex questions, such as DNA evidence and psychological theory, will continue to irritate experts and lawyers. And questions of racial bias and other prejudices will continue to drive debates about jury composition and the abuse of voir dire (the jury selection process).

Still, after some one thousand years this medieval institution has shown a surprising resilience and vitality. Through popular television shows like *Law and Order* and best sellers by John Grisham and others, not to mention real-life celebrity trials, millions of Americans who will never sit in a jury box have a fairly good sense of the great duties and powers of juries. If anything, it is harder today to imagine an America without trial by jury than it was for the Founders, who fought so hard to protect this right and to guarantee that Americans would forever enjoy this measure of direct democracy.

CHAPTER ONE

Trial by Jury Becomes a Fundamental American Right

The Medieval Origins
of Trial by Jury

Leonard W. Levy

Leonard W. Levy is the Pulitzer Prize–winning author of *Origins of the Fifth Amendment: The Right Against Self-Incrimination, Original Intent and the Framers' Constitution*, and numerous other works on constitutional history. He was formerly the Earl Warren Professor of Constitutional History at Brandeis University and a professor of humanities and history at the Claremont Graduate School. In the section below he describes the origins of the right to trial by jury in the Middle Ages. Surprisingly for this bulwark of individual liberty, trial by jury grew out of a desire by English kings, particularly Henry II, to assert their authority and protect their prerogatives. In England, the royal "inquest" slowly began to replace primitive trial methods, such as trial by ordeal or battle, which were common throughout Europe in the Dark Ages. Eventually, the peculiar forms of the inquest, including the formal presentment of charges and the questioning of a representative group, grew into the grand and petty juries that exist today. Originally a group of witnesses, chosen because of their familiarity with the defendant or the matter under dispute, the jurors gradually became the impartial arbiters of truth.

———

Trial by jury is the mainstay of the accusatorial system of criminal justice. Accusatorial procedure antedated the Norman Conquest [of England in 1066]. From the early Middle Ages, civil and ecclesiastical authorities throughout western Europe had employed substantially similar accusatorial

Leonard W. Levy, *The Palladium of Justice: Origins of Trial by Jury*. Chicago: Ivan R. Dee, 1999. Copyright © 1999 by Leonard W. Levy. Reproduced by permission of the publisher.

procedures. The latter half of the twelfth century and the first half of the thirteenth was a period of transition that witnessed profound transformations of procedure. Old forms of trial, once universal, broke down and newer ones emerged. In England the new forms, presentment (the formal statement of an offense, presented to authority) and trial by jury, preserved the accusatorial character of the old; on the Continent and in the ecclesiastical courts, inquisitorial procedure was triumphant. By no coincidence, the liberties of the subject were to thrive in England and be throttled on the Continent.

Community courts and community justice prevailed in England at the time of the Norman Conquest. The legal system was ritualistic, dependent upon oaths at most stages of litigation, and permeated by both religious and superstitious notions. Legal concepts were so primitive that no distinction existed between civil and criminal cases or between secular and ecclesiastical cases. Proceedings were oral, very personal, and highly confrontative. Juries were unknown. One party publicly "appealed," or accused, the other in front of a community meeting at which the presence of both was obligatory. Absence meant risking fines and outlawry. After the preliminary statements of the parties, the court rendered judgment, not on the merits of the issue or the question of guilt or innocence, but on the manner by which it should be resolved. Judgment, in other words, preceded trial, because it was a decision on what form the trial should take. It might be by compurgation [sworn character witnesses], by ordeal, or, after the Norman Conquest, by battle. Excepting trial by battle, only one party was tried or, more accurately, was put to his "proof." Proof being regarded as an advantage, it was usually awarded to the accused party; in effect, he had the privilege of proving his own case.

Trial by exculpatory oath and compurgation, also called canonical purgation, consisted of a sworn statement to the truth of one's claim or denial, supported by the oaths of a certain number of fellow swearers. Presumably they would not endanger their immortal souls by the sacrilege of false swearing. Originally the oath-helpers swore from their own knowledge to the truth of the party's claim. Later they became little more than character witnesses, swearing only to their belief that his oath was trustworthy. If he rounded up the requisite number of compurgators and the cumbrous swearing in very exact form proceeded without a mistake, he won his case. A mistake "burst" the oath, proving guilt.

Ordeals were usually reserved for more serious crimes, for persons of bad reputation, for peasants, or for those caught with stolen goods. As an invocation of immediate divine judgment, ordeals were consecrated by the church and shrouded with solemn religious mystery. The accused underwent a physical trial in which he called upon God to witness his innocence by putting a miraculous sign upon his body. Cold water, boiling water, and hot iron were the principal ordeals, all of which the clergy administered. In the ordeal of cold water, the accused was trussed up and cast into a pool to see whether he would sink or float. On the theory that water which had been sanctified by a priest would receive an innocent person but reject the guilty, innocence was proved by sinking—and with luck a quick retrieval; guilt was proved by floating. In the other ordeals, one had to plunge his hand into a cauldron of boiling water or carry a red-hot piece of iron for a certain distance, in the hope that three days later, when the bandages were removed, a priest would find a "clean" wound, one that was healing free of infection. How deeply one plunged his arm into the water, how heavy the iron or great the distance it was carried, depended mainly on the gravity of the charge.

The Normans brought to England still another ordeal, trial by battle, paradigm of the adversary system, which gave to the legal concept of "defense" or "defendant" a physical meaning. Trial by battle was a savage yet sacred method of proof which was also thought to involve divine intercession on behalf of the righteous. Rather than let a wrongdoer triumph, God would presumably strengthen the arms of the party who had sworn truly to the justice of his cause. Right, not might, would therefore conquer. Trial by battle was originally available for the settlement of all disputes, from debt and ownership to robbery and rape, but eventually was restricted to cases of serious crime. In this particular form of proof there was a significant exception to the oral character of the old procedures. The accusation leading to battle, technically known as an "appeal of felony," had to be written, and nothing but the most exact form, giving full particulars of the alleged crime, would be accepted. The indictment, or accusation, by grand jury would later imitate the "appeal" in this respect.

Whether one proved his case by compurgation, ordeal, or battle, the method was accusatory in character. There was always a definite and known accuser, some private person who brought formal suit and openly confronted his antagonist. There was never any secrecy in the proceedings, which were the same for criminal as for civil litigation. The judges, who had no role whatever in the making of the verdict, decided only which party should be put to proof and what its form should be; thereafter the judges merely enforced an observance of the rules. The oaths that saturated the proceedings called upon God to witness to the truth of the respective claims of the parties, or the justice of their cause, or the reliability of their word. No one gave testimonial evidence, nor was anyone questioned to test his veracity.

The Inquest

It was the inquest, a radically different proceeding, that eventually supplanted the old forms of proof while borrowing their accusatorial character. An extraordinarily fertile and versatile device, the inquest was the parent of our double jury system, the grand jury of accusation and the petty jury of trial. Fortunately for the history of freedom, the inquest, a Norman import, was also one of the principal means by which the monarchy developed a centralized government in England. The survival of the inquest was insured by its close ties to royal power and royal prosperity; its particular English form was founded on the old accusatorial procedures. The word "inquest" derives from the Latin *inquisitio*, or inquisition, but beyond the similarity in name shared nothing with the canon law procedure, which became, in fact, its opposite and great rival. The inquest was also known as the *recognitio*, or recognition, which meant a solemn answer or finding or declaration of truth. The inquest was just that, an answer or declaration of truth, a *veri dictum*, or verdict by a body of men from the same neighborhood who were summoned by some official, on the authority of the crown, to reply under oath to any inquiries that might be addressed to them. Men of the same locality were chosen simply because they were most likely to know best the answers to questions relating to the inquest—who had evaded taxes, who owned certain lands, who was suspected of crime, and who knew of misconduct among the king's officers. . . .

Reforms of Henry II

What was an irregular and in some respects an extraordinary procedure became under King Henry II (1154–1189) normal and systematic. A man of powerful will, administrative genius, and reforming spirit, Henry II greatly increased the jurisdiction of the royal courts, and wherever they traveled on eyre [circuit] through the kingdom, the inquest followed. Henry II disliked and distrusted the traditional forms of proof. More boldly than his predecessors, he regarded breaches of peace or threats to life and limb as offenses of a public nature, warranting more than merely private retribution. Crimes of a serious nature he took to be offenses against the king's peace, requiring settlement in the king's courts by the king's system of justice, whenever possible, rather than by the older proofs only; and the king's system was founded on the inquest, the representative verdict of the neighborhood. What was once only an administrative inquiry became the foundation of the jury of accusation and the jury of trial in both civil and criminal matters. . . .

Henry II did not abolish older forms of proof; he sought, instead, to supersede them in as many instances as possible, by discrediting them and by making available to litigants an alternative and more equitable form of proceeding. Innovations began in 1164 when the Constitutions of Clarendon prescribed the use of a recognition by twelve sworn men to decide any dispute between laymen and clergy on the question whether land was subject to lay or clerical tenure. The Constitutions of Clarendon provided also that laymen should not be sued in ecclesiastical courts on untrustworthy or insufficient evidence, but that if the suspect were someone whom no one might dare to accuse, the sheriff on the request of the bishop must swear a jury of twelve to declare the truth by bringing the accusation. In the Constitutions of Clarendon, then, one sees the glimmering of the civil jury in cases of land disputes and of the grand jury of criminal presentment or accusation.

Origins of the Grand Jury

The Assize, or ordinance, of Clarendon, which Henry II promulgated two years later, on the centennial of the Conquest, provided for the firm foundation of the grand jury and instituted a variety of significant procedural reforms. The king instructed the royal judges on circuit, or eyre, to take jurisdiction over certain serious crimes or felonies presented to them by sworn inquests, the representative juries of the various localities. Twelve men from each hundred of the county and four from each vill or township of the hundred were to be summoned by the sheriff to attend the public eyre. They were enjoined to inquire into all crimes since the beginning of Henry II's reign, and to report under oath all persons accused or suspected by the vicinage. The parties who were thus presented, if not already in custody, would be arrested and put to the ordeal of cold water. Even if absolved, those of very bad reputation were forced to leave the realm. In certain cases, then, mere presentment was tantamount to a verdict of banishment, but generally was not more than an accusation that was tried by ordeal. The Assize of Northampton, issued in 1176, recodified the Assize of Clarendon, extended the list of felonies, and substituted maiming for hanging as the punishment of the accused felon who was "undone" at the ordeal; he also lost a foot, his right hand, his chattels, and was banished. In actuality he usually fled to the forest if he could to live as an outlaw to escape the ordeal or banishment. The Assize of 1176 made permanent, at least at the pleasure of the king, the revised procedure of accusation by twelve knights of the hundred or twelve freemen of the hundred and four of the vill.

The Assizes of Clarendon and Northampton, by establishing what became the grand jury, offered a royally sanctioned option to the old system of private accusations by appeals of felony. Trial by battle, which was begun by an "appeal of felony" in criminal cases, continued, but it was undermined by the king's jury of criminal presentment as the model way of beginning a criminal trial. . . .

Civil Juries

Reform of the machinery of civil justice at the expense of trial by battle was one of Henry II's foremost achievements. Once again his instrument was the sworn inquest or jury. Its use in cases of property disputes contributed to the stability of land tenures, extended the jurisdiction of the royal courts at the expense of the feudal courts, aided the cause of justice at the same time that fees for the privilege of using the royal courts contributed to the king's exchequer, and sapped trial by battle in civil cases. The Constitutions of Clarendon in 1164 provided the precedent for turning to twelve men of the countryside for a verdict on a question concerning property rights. Such questions, especially in relation to the possession and title of land, produced the most common and surely the most important civil actions. For their solution Henry II gradually introduced what became the trial jury.

In 1166 the assize of *novel disseisin*, or recent dispossession, established the principle that no one might be evicted or dispossessed of his land without the approval of a jury verdict. This assize created a legal remedy for one who had been dispossessed. He could obtain a writ commanding the sheriff to summon twelve freemen of the vicinity who presumably knew the facts of the case, put them under oath, and then in the presence of the itinerant royal judges require them to render a verdict on the question whether the tenant had been dispossessed. A verdict in the tenant's favor restored him to possession of his land. If, however, a lord seized the land of a tenant who died before the tenant's heirs might take possession of it, the assize of *novel disseisin* provided no remedy. The assize of *mort d'ancestor*, instituted in 1176, did so. The heir might obtain a writ that put before a jury the question whether the decedent died in possession of the land and whether the claimant was his rightful heir. In the same reign, the assize of *darrein presentment* provided for a verdict by jury on questions involving rival claims to the possession of certain "advowsons," or ecclesiastical benefices, which were regarded as a form of real estate. . . .

By the time of Magna Carta in 1215, the inquest in civil cases was becoming fairly well established as the trial jury, though in criminal cases it was scarcely known at all. The petty or possessory assizes of *novel disseisin, mort d'ancestor*, and *darrein presentment* had proved to be so popular that chapter eighteen of Magna Carta guaranteed that the circuit court would sit several times a year in each county for the purpose of obtaining verdicts on disputes that they settled. Civil disputes of virtually any description, not merely those named in the petty assizes, might be referred to the verdict of local recognitors if both parties would consent to the procedure.

Juries and Criminal Cases

On the criminal side of the law, Magna Carta in chapter thirty-six provided that the writ *de odio et atia*, which by 1215 had become known as the writ of life and limb, should be granted without charge. It was by no means uncommon by then for a person accused by private appeal to demand a jury verdict on any number of "exceptions," such as the writ of life and limb, in the hope of getting the appeal quashed. In such cases, however, the jury decided only the question whether the "exception" was valid; the main question of guilt or innocence, which the appeal had raised, was still settled by battle if the exception was not sustained. Criminal accusations, which were presented in accord with the grand inquest provided by the Assize of Clarendon, were tried by ordeal. Magna Carta, in chapter twenty-eight, ensured that no one could be put to the ordeal unless formally accused by the jury of presentment before the royal judges on circuit. This was the implication of the provision that "credible witnesses," members of the presenting jury, must corroborate that fact that there had been an indictment. The celebrated chapter twenty-nine did not guarantee trial by jury for the simple reason that its use in criminal cases was still unknown in 1215. At best that chapter ensured that the indictment and trial by whatever was the appropriate test, whether battle or ordeal, must precede sentence.

The course of history was affected at the same time by events in Rome. The Fourth Lateran Council in 1215 forbade the participation of the clergy in the administration of ordeals, thereby divesting that proof of its rationale as a judgment of God. As a result, the ordeal died as a form of trial in western Europe, and some other procedure was needed to take its place. . . .

With the ordeal abolished, battle remained the only means of trying a criminal case. But the movement of the law was away from battle. The same reasons of "equity" that led [Ranulf de] Glanville [chief justice to Henry II] in 1187 to say that the right to a freehold "can scarcely be proved by battle" spurred the search for an alternate means of proving an accusation of crime. Thus Magna Carta had made the writ of life and limb free but still reflected traditional thinking in terms of ordeals and battle. Battle could never be had, however, in cases where one of the parties was aged, crippled, sick, or a woman. . . .

Not only was there no way to try those who could not engage in battle; there was the greater quandary of what should be done with persons who had been accused by the sworn verdict of a grand inquest. Battle was possible only in the case of a private appeal of felony. According to [Sir James Fitzjames] Stephen, "When trial by ordeal was abolished and the system of accusation by grand juries was established, absolutely no mode of ascertaining the truth of an accusation made by a grand jury remained." Nevertheless, compurgation and suit by witnesses lingered for a long time.

The crown's bewilderment was revealed in a writ of 1219 giving instructions to the circuit judges: "Because it was in doubt and not definitely settled before the beginning of your eyre, with what trial those are to be judged who are accused of robbery, murder, arson, and similar crimes, since the trial by fire and water has been prohibited by the Roman Church," notorious criminals should be imprisoned, those accused of "medium" crimes who were not likely to offend again should be banished, and those accused of lesser crimes might be released on "pledge of fidelity and keeping our peace." The writ concluded, "We have left to your discretion the observance of this aforesaid order according to your own discretion and conscience," a formula that left the judges further perplexed but free to improvise.

Origins of the Petty Jury

Treating an accusation as a conviction, when an accusation was little more than an expression of popular opinion, was a makeshift that fell so short of doing justice that it could not survive. In retrospect it seems natural that the judges on circuit should have turned to a sworn inquest for help. An eyre was a great event, virtually a county parliament. Present were the local nobles and bishops, the sheriffs and bailiffs, the knights and freeholders, and a very great many juries. From every hundred of the county there was a jury of twelve men, and from every township four representatives. Surrounded by the various juries, the judge in a criminal case could take the obvious course of seeking the sense of the community. The original jury of presentment was already sworn, presumably knew most about the facts, and was a representative group. The jurors' indictment had not necessarily voiced their own belief in the prisoner's guilt; it rather affirmed the fact that he was commonly suspected. Although practice varied considerably at first, the judges began to ask the jury of presentment to render a verdict of guilty or not guilty on their accusation. Because the jury of presentment was more likely than not to sustain its indictment, even though the jurors had sworn only that the accused was suspected and not that he was guilty, the judges usually swore in the representatives of the surrounding townships and asked whether they concurred; the jury of another hundred might also be conscripted to corroborate the verdict. In effect a body of the countryside gave the verdict.

This practice of enlarging the original jury of presentment or seeking a series of verdicts from different juries was common during the thirteenth century. What became the petty jury was thus initially larger than the grand jury. The practice was too cumbersome, the body too unwieldy. Twelve was the number of the presenting jury and twelve the jury in many civil cases; gradually only twelve jurors were selected to try the indictment, but they always included among their number some of the original jury of presentment. The unfairness inherent in this practice, and the theory that the accused must consent to this jury, eventually led to a complete separation of the grand jury and the trial jury.

Consent and the Petty Jury

Consent, even if induced by coercion, was an ancient feature of accusatory procedure. . . . But no man would be likely to consent to the verdict of accusers if they sought his conviction. And no man, it was thought, should be forced to accept the verdict of accusers; acceptance should be voluntary. While ordeals were still in use, if an accused refused to submit himself to the proof, he was considered to have repudiated the law and might therefore be punished as if he had outlawed himself. But the inquest acting as a trial jury was a novel and extraordinary device, and thus the reasoning that had branded as outlaws those who rejected the ordeal now seemed repugnant when it was applied to a man who refused to put himself to the test of a jury. He might think the jury would not fairly decide, or that his chances of getting a verdict of not guilty, for whatever reasons, were hopeless. . . .

In cases of no consent, some judges proceeded with the trial anyway; others treated the prisoner as if he were guilty; but most felt that it was unreasonable to compel a man to submit unless he consented. If he refused to consent, the law was nonplussed, the proceedings stymied. At length, in 1275 a statute supplied the answer: extort his consent. The statute read, "that notorious felons who are openly of evil fame and who refuse to put themselves upon inquests of felony at the suit of the King before his justices, shall be remanded to a hard and strong prison as befits those who refuse to abide by the common law of the land; but this is not to be understood of persons who are taken upon light suspicion." . . .

The other path taken by the notion of consent led to the emergence of the petty jury in criminal cases. This was the outcome of permitting the prisoner to challenge members of the presenting jury who were impaneled to serve on his trial jury. . . . With increasing frequency defendants challenged petty jurors who had first served as their indictors, though the king's justices resisted the challenges because indictors were more likely to convict. For that very reason in the 1340s the Commons twice protested against the inclusion of indictors, but it was not until 1352 that the king agreed to a statute that gave the accused a right to challenge members of the petty jury who had participated in his indictment. As a result of this statute, the two juries became differentiated in composition and function. From about 1376 the custom of requiring a unanimous verdict from twelve petty jurors developed; by that time the size of the grand jury had been fixed at twenty-three, a majority of whom decided whether accusations should be proffered.

A Fair Trial, for Its Time

By the middle of the fifteenth century, criminal trials were being conducted by rational principles that seem quite modern. Although the law of evidence was still in its rudimentary stages, the trial jury was no longer regarded as a band of witnesses, men who of their own knowledge or from knowledge immediately available from the neighborhood, might swear to the guilt or innocence of the accused. The jury was beginning to hear evidence that was produced in court, though the jurors still continued to obtain facts by their own inquiry. As late as the 1450s it was common for the jurors to visit a witness at his home in the country to take his testimony, but they were also beginning to pass judgment on evidence given in their presence in court. More important, they were regarded as a body of objective men, triers of fact, whose verdict was based on the truth as best they could determine it. . . .

Of course, trial by the local community could be trial by local prejudice, but at least the prisoner knew the charges against him, confronted his accuser, and had freedom to give his own explanations as well as question and argue with the prosecution's witnesses. He suffered from many disadvantages—lack of counsel, lack of witnesses on his own behalf, lack of time to prepare his defense—yet the trial was supremely fair, judged by any standard known in the Western world of that day.

The Colonies Embrace Trial by Jury

Francis H. Heller

Francis H. Heller, a longtime law and political science professor at the University of Kansas, has written numerous studies on constitutional law and history, including a comprehensive study of the Sixth Amendment, excerpted below. As Heller explains, the colonists arrived in the New World with the "full rights of Englishmen," including the right to jury trials. At first, primitive conditions and a hostility to lawyers led to more informality in the colonial systems of justice, but eventually England reasserted its control over the colonies and English-trained lawyers began to dominate colonial courts. These lawyers brought with them new concepts of defendants' rights, and the colonial governments began instituting these rights, although somewhat inconsistently. After the Revolutionary War, the new states retained this diversity, and for this reason the Constitutional Convention included a right to trial by jury in the Constitution but left the details rather vague.

———————

That the English law should follow the colonists to their new homes was apparently intended by the Crown, for the Elizabethan patents to [explorers Humphrey] Gilbert and [Walter] Raleigh already contain statements to the effect that the colonists settled under these grants should possess the same constitutional rights as were enjoyed by Englishmen in the homeland. The first Virginia charter by James I in 1606, recited that

Francis H. Heller, *The Sixth Amendment to the Constitution of the United States: A Study in Constitutional Development.* Lawrence: University of Kansas Press, 1951. Copyright © 1951 by the University of Kansas Press. Reproduced by permission.

we do for Us, our Heirs and Successors, Declare by these Presents, that all and every the Persons, being our Subjects, which shall dwell and inhabit within every or any of the several Colonies and Plantations, and every of their children, which shall happen to be born within any of the Limits and Precincts of the said several Colonies and Plantations, shall HAVE and enjoy all Liberties, Franchises, and Immunities, within any of our other Dominions, to all Intents and Purposes, as if they had been abiding and born, within this our Realm of *England*, or any other of our said Dominions.

Similar language may be found in most of the later charters.

Trials as a Right of Englishmen

Among the rights of Englishmen, trial by jury had by then won undeniable recognition. Indeed, until Brunner's researches[1] exploded the theory, it was generally believed that trial by jury was an institution of such long standing as to antedate the Great Charter of King John. Thus, e.g., [Supreme Court Justice Joseph] Story, in an oft-quoted passage, asserted that

It seems hardly necessary in this place to expatiate upon the antiquity or importance of the trial by jury in criminal cases. It was from very early times insisted on by our ancestors in the parent country, as the great bulwark of their civil and political liberties, and watched with an unceasing jealousy and solicitude. The right constitutes one of the fundamental articles of Magna Charta, in which it is declared, "*nullus homo capiatur, nec imprisonetur, aut exulet, aut aliquo modo destruatur, etc.; nisi per legale judicium parium suorum, vel per legem terrae;*" no man shall be arrested, nor imprisoned, nor banished, nor deprived of life, etc., but by the judgment of his peers, or by the law of the land. The judgment of his peers here alluded to, and commonly called in the quaint language of former times a trial

1. Heinrich Brunner, *Die Entstehung der Schwurgerichte*, 1872.

per pais, or trial by the country, is the trial by jury, who are called the peers of the party accused, being of the like condition and equality in the state. When our more immediate ancestors removed to America, they brought this great privilege with them, as their birthright and inheritance, as a part of that admirable common law, which had fenced round and interposed barriers on every side against the approaches of arbitrary power.

We know today that this statement was doubly in error. It appears well established at present that trial by jury was not known in its present form or function when the barons forced King John's signature [of the Magna Carta] at Runnymede. This, however, does not diminish the significance of the belief generally held in the seventeenth and eighteenth centuries that trial by jury was among the fundamental rights guaranteed by the Great Charter. Considering the almost religious veneration accorded to that document by the great majority of the people both in England and in this country, it is more important to recognize the fact that our ancestors associated trial by jury with this renowned mainspring of liberty than to insist that in so doing they were guilty of historical error.

Informality of Colonial Justice

It may be more significant that modern research has led to another correction of Justice Story's statement. The varied reception which trial by jury received among the early colonists took on added significance as historical scholarship compelled a reexamination of the traditional juristic theory which assumes a wholesale transfer of the common law from the mother country to the colonies. Thus the development of jury trial in America reflects the fact that there was at first . . . an attempt by laymen to order their affairs by themselves in an atmosphere of pronounced hostility toward the legal profession and their methods. The jury trial of colonial days is, therefore, not a rigid copy of its English prototype but rather the result of variegated experiences, experimentation, and adaptation. The different practices so established were sufficiently divergent to allow only the most general statement with regard to jury trial to be included in the Constitution framed at Philadelphia, lest local customs be offended.

Juries were impanelled from the earliest period on. [One historian,] after extensive research in the *Massachusetts Colonial Records*, found evidence of a jury trial a few months after [Massachusetts Colonial Governor John] Winthrop's arrival. And the only extant item of legislation of the first five years of the Plymouth Colony is an ordinance of 1623 which provides among other things "that all criminal facts . . . shall be tried by the verdict of twelve honest men, to be impanelled by authority, in form of a jury upon their oaths." The Massachusetts Body of Liberties (1641) confirms this public policy with the declaration in Article 29 that "in all actions at law, it shall be the libertie of the plaintiff and the defendant, by mutual consent, to choose whether they will be tried by the Bench or by a Jurie . . . the like libertie shall be granted to all persons in Criminal cases." But the system was by no means unquestionably accepted and, for a time, seems to have had a very insecure tenure. Thus only one year after its apparent guarantee in the Body of Liberties the retention or rejection of jury trial was the subject of a special commission of inquiry; and it seems that juries may even have been abolished for a time, as a 1652 resolve decrees that "the law about juries is repealed and juries are in force again." . . .

More details are available to the general reader with regard to the administration of justice in colonial Virginia than any other of the New World settlements. These accounts further illustrate the informality of the early period, the temporary emergence of popular, nontechnical justice, accompanied as in the other colonies by manifestations of strong opposition against the professional lawyer. The courts of Virginia initially exercised many powers and discharged many duties of a nonjudicial character, a practice which even today has not entirely disappeared. On the other hand, the legislative branch of the colonial government was equally ready to exercise judicial functions. Thus the first House of Burgesses on August 3, 1619, heard and adjudged a criminal complaint by Captain William Powell against his servant Thomas Garnett. Nor were the proceedings in the courts of Virginia always in full conformity with the law of England. Although the Instructions of King James (1606) provided specifically that in all capital cases the question of guilt or innocence should be decided by "twelve honest and indifferent persons sworn upon the Evangelists," we find in 1630 trials being conducted before juries of thirteen and fourteen members. More importantly, jury trials in Virginia differed from those in the mother country with respect to the requirement that the jury be drawn from the vicinage. As all cases involving loss of life or limb had to be tried before the General Court in Jamestown, it was frequently difficult, if not impossible, to secure jurors from the neighborhood where the crime had been committed. For some time, the jury seems to have been selected from among the bystanders at the court at Jamestown, but by statute (2 Hen. 63–64) in 1662 the problem was met by providing that the sheriff of the accused's county was to summon six freeholders from the neighborhood or jury service (for the inducive fee of twenty pounds of tobacco per day), while the other six members of the panel would be selected from the court's bystanders as had been the custom. A strict property qualification further limited the number of those eligibles for jury service.

A New Formality and New Rights

The consolidation of governmental power in the colonies which was generally accomplished in the closing years of the seventeenth century and during the reign of Queen Anne [1702–1714] also brought about greater stability in the administration of justice. Professional lawyers assumed their place and gained recognition in colonial society. Except in Delaware, the bench, as in England, became the exclusive domain of those trained in the law. Many of those lawyers had received their training at the Inns of Court in London and brought with them, applied, and enforced the procedural modifications enacted in England after the Revolution of 1688. Thus these reforms, the new liberality as to witnesses and counsel for the accused, became associated in the minds of the people with the aims of greater freedom that had caused the overthrow of the Stuarts [Charles I and

James II] and [the pro-monarchy] Tories. No longer could the royal prerogative overawe the courts; indeed, it was the aim now, as declared for Pennsylvania, "that all Criminals shall have the same Privileges of Witnesses and Council [*sic*] as their Prosecutors."

The Public Prosecutor: A Colonial Innovation

To the American colonists the meaning of this sentence was not what it would have been to their English cousins. For early in the eighteenth century the American system of judicial administration adopted an institution which was (and to some extent still is) unknown in England: while rejecting the fundamental juristic concepts upon which continental Europe's inquisitorial system of criminal procedure is predicated, the colonies borrowed one of its institutions, the public prosecutor, and grafted it upon the body of English (accusatorial) procedure embodied in the common law. Presumably, this innovation was brought about by the lack of lawyers, particularly in the newly settled regions, and by the increasing distances between the colonial capitals on the eastern seaboard and the ever-receding western frontier. Its result was that, at a time when virtually all but treason trials in England were still in the nature of suits between private parties, the accused in the colonies faced a government official whose specific function it was to prosecute, and who was incomparably more familiar than the accused with the problems of procedure, the idiosyncrasies of juries, and, last but not least, the personnel of the court. The balance would continue to be weighted in favor of the Crown unless extreme vigilance was practiced to safeguard the precarious privileges so recently granted to the accused.

Thus when the Continental Congress declared "that the respective colonies are entitled to the common law, and more especially to the great and inestimable privilege of being tried by their peers of the vicinage, according to the course of that law," the common law so appealed to must be understood to include not only trial by a jury of twelve men of the vicinage but also publicity of the proceedings, and the right to witnesses and to the assistance of counsel; in short, all the recognized rights of the accused. The denial of these rights was among the grievances complained of in the Declaration of Independence. The inviolability of these rights was asserted in the constitutional documents of most of the new states, which, while differing in details and degree of emphasis, sounded a common note in including, among the fundamental rights of the individual, guarantees against arbitrary practices in criminal proceedings, safeguards to counteract the might of government when it called the individual lawbreaker before the bar of justice.

Variation in the States

The Declaration of Rights of the new state of Maryland (1776), after reiterating, in language borrowed from the Continental Congress's declaration of 1774, the right of its inhabitants to the common law of England and trial by jury, proclaimed "that the trial of facts where they arise, is one of the greatest securities of the lives, liberties and estates of the people," and then enumerated the rights which every man had in criminal proceedings: to be informed of the accusation against him; to receive a copy of the indictment in time to permit him to prepare his defense; to be allowed counsel; to be confronted with the witnesses against him; to have process for his own witnesses; to examine the witnesses, for and against him, on oath; and to have "a speedy trial by an impartial jury, without whose unanimous consent he ought not to be found guilty." . . .

South Carolina furnishes a telling example of the high esteem in which Magna Carta was held at the time, in a single brief article of its constitution which obviously was intended to parallel the wording of the Great Charter:

> That no freeman of this State be taken or imprisoned, or disseized of his freehold, liberties or privileges, or outlawed, exiled, or deprived of his life, liberty, or property, but by the judgment of his peers or by the law of the land. . . .

The most detailed provisions are those contained in the Declaration of Rights of Massachusetts (1780) and the largely identical language of the Bill of Rights of New Hampshire (1784). Elaborately and circumspectly phrased, these documents in essence guaranteed the accused the right to know the nature of the accusation, to decline self-incrimination, to present his own evidence, to meet the witnesses against him, and to have the assistance of counsel; and in words that hark back to Magna Carta they reaffirmed the right to trial by jury or by the law of the land. In each instance, a separate article limited criminal trials to the vicinity where the alleged offense had taken place.

Reluctance to Override States at Constitutional Convention

The New Hampshire articles numbered almost three hundred words; while South Carolina used less than fifty words to cover the same subject. This numerical difference alone is indicative of the diversity of substance to be found among the several states. As the perception and interpretation of the common law varied in the several states, as criminal procedures were more or less fair or arbitrary, so differed the sense of urgency with which the inhabitants of the different states viewed the problem of protecting the accused. Hence it is not surprising that the delegates who convened at Philadelphia in the spring of 1787 made no effort to embody details of criminal procedure in the document they were about to propose to the nation. The original Virginia Plan contained no references whatsoever to the procedure to be had in criminal cases. The New Jersey Plan, however, with an eye toward the preservation of the rights of the states in judicial matters, proposed

> that no person shall be liable to be tried for any criminal offense, committed within any of the United States, in any other state than that wherein the offense shall be committed, nor be deprived of the privilege of trial by jury, by virtue of any law of the United States.

A similar provision was included in Alexander Hamilton's draft; and [South Carolina representative Charles] Pinckney's outline suggested the same two guarantees, and in addition would have stipulated that trials should be open and public.

The Committee on Detail adopted the essence of these suggestions and embodied them in its draft constitution as section 4 of Article XI, in language resembling Pinckney's draft:

The trial of criminal offences (except in cases of impeachment) shall be in the State where they shall be committed; and shall be by Jury.

Without much debate, this section was amended in Committee of the Whole in order to "provide for trial by jury of offenses committed out of any State." It was in this amended form that the provision was sent to the Committee on Style, which, without further change, incorporated it in the Judiciary Article of the final document as the third clause of the second section.

The Constitution Threatens Trial by Jury

Part I: "Federal Farmer"; Part II: Pennsylvania Delegation Minority

In deference to the strong beliefs of the American people, the framers of the Constitution included the right to trial by jury in criminal cases in Article III, Section 2, one of the few individual rights to be included in the original draft of the Constitution. Oddly enough, this very inclusion raised suspicions in the minds of some of the Anti-Federalists, the opponents of ratification, who worried that specifying this right in criminal trials actually threatened the same right in civil cases. Among these critics was an anonymous person who called himself "Federal Farmer," whose letters were published in the *Poughkeepsie County Journal* (in New York) from October 1787 to January 1788. Part I of the following selection was excerpted from one such letter dated October 12, 1787. In addition to raising concerns about defendants' rights, the author contends that federal jurisdiction will downgrade local juries by requiring cases to be decided far from the events in question. The author of these sentiments, shared by a number of Anti-Federalists, was long thought to have been Richard Henry Lee, the Virginia delegate to the Continental Congress who introduced the resolution calling for independence from Great Britain. Federal Farmer may instead have been Melancton Smith, a prominent Anti-Federalist leader in New York, or possibly a collaboration between both men. Part II of the following viewpoint was taken from a "Dissent" signed by twenty-one delegates to Pennsylvania's ratifying convention and published in the *Pennsylvania Packet* on December 18, 1787. The dissenters lay out their

Bernard Bailyn, ed., *The Debate on the Constitution: Federalist and Antifederalist Speeches, Articles, and Letters During the Struggle over Ratification.* New York: The Library of America, 1993.

most serious objections to the Constitution, including their belief that federal courts could usurp the right of juries to establish the facts of a case and that these courts could also blur the lines between civil and criminal cases, allowing even criminal cases to proceed without benefit of juries. Due to the concerns of Anti-Federalists such as Federal Farmer and the Pennsylvania dissenters, the right to a trial by jury in both criminal and civil cases was subsequently codified in Amendments VI and VII, respectively, of the Bill of Rights.

I

If there are a number of rights established by the state constitutions, and which will remain sacred, and the general government is bound to take notice of them—it must take notice of one as well as another; and if unnecessary to recognize or establish one by the federal constitution, it would be unnecessary to recognize or establish another by it. If the federal constitution is to be construed so far in connection with the state constitutions, as to leave the trial by jury in civil causes, for instance, secured; on the same principles it would have left the trial by jury in criminal causes, the benefits of the writ of habeas corpus, &c. secured; they all stand on the same footing; they are the common rights of Americans, and have been recognized by the state constitutions: But the convention found it necessary to recognize or re-establish the benefits of that writ, and the jury trial in criminal cases. . . .

The trials by jury in civil causes, it is said, varies so much in several states, that no words could be found for the uniform establishment of it. If so the federal legislation will not be able to establish it by any general laws. I confess I am of opinion it may be established, but not in that beneficial manner in which we may enjoy it. . . . When I speak of the jury trial of the vicinage, or the trial of the fact in the neighbourhood,—I do not lay so much stress upon the circumstance of our being tried by our neighbours: in this enlightened country men may be probably impartially tried by those who do not live very near them: but the trial of facts in the neighbourhood is of great importance in other respects. Nothing can be more essential than the cross examining witnesses, and generally before the triers of the facts in question. The common people can establish facts with much more ease with oral than written evidence; when trials of facts are removed to a distance from the homes of the parties and witnesses, oral evidence becomes intolerably expensive, and the parties must depend on written evidence, which to the common people is expensive and almost useless, it must be frequently taken ex-parte [from one side only], and but very seldom leads to the proper discovery of truth.

Juries Give Influence to Common People

The trial by jury is very important in another point of view. It is essential in every free country, that common people should have a part and share of influence, in the judicial as well as in the legislative department. To hold open to them the offices of senators, judges, and officers to fill which an expensive education is required, cannot answer any valuable purposes for them; they are not in a situation to be brought forward and to fill those offices; these, and most other offices of any considerable importance, will be occupied by the few. The few, the well born, &c. as Mr. [John] Adams calls them, in judicial decisions as well as in legislation, are generally disposed, and very naturally too, to favour those of their own description.

The trial by jury in the judicial department, and the collection of the people by their representatives in the legislature, are those fortunate inventions which have procured for them in this country, their true proportion of influence, and the wisest and most fit means of protecting themselves in the community. Their situation, as jurors and representatives, enables them to acquire information and knowledge in the affairs and government of the society; and to come forward, in turn, as the centinels and guardians of each other. I am very sorry that even a few of our countrymen should consider jurors and representatives in a different point of view, as ignorant, troublesome bodies, which ought not to have any share in the concerns of government.

II

The judicial power, under the proposed constitution, is founded on the well-known principles of the *civil law*, by which the judge determines both on law and fact, and appeals are allowed from the inferior tribunals to the superior, upon the whole question; so that *facts* as well as *law*, would be re-examined, and even new facts brought forward in the court of appeals; and to use the words of a very eminent Civilian—"The cause is many times another thing before the court of appeals, than what it was at the time of the first sentence."

That this mode of proceeding is the one which must be adopted under this constitution, is evident from the following circumstances:—1st. That the trial by jury, which is the grand characteristic of the common law, is secured by the constitution, only in criminal cases.—2d. That the appeal from both *law* and *fact* is expressly established, which is utterly inconsistent with the principles of the common law, and trials by jury. The only mode in which an appeal from law and fact can be established, is, by adopting the principles and practice of the civil law; unless the United States should be drawn into the absurdity of calling and swearing juries, merely for the purpose of contradicting their verdicts, which would render juries contemptible and worse than useless.— 3d. That the courts to be established would decide on all cases *of law and equity*, which is a well known characteristic of the civil law, and these courts would have conusance not only of the laws of the United States and of treaties, and of cases affecting ambassadors, but of all cases of *admiralty and maritime jurisdiction*, which last are matters belonging exclusively to the civil law, in every nation in Christendom.

"Monstrous Expence" of Appeals Process

Not to enlarge upon the loss of the invaluable right of trial by an unbiassed jury, so dear to every friend of liberty, the monstrous expence and inconveniences of the mode of proceeding to be adopted, are such as will prove intolerable to the people of this country. The lengthy proceedings of the civil law courts in the chancery of England, and in the courts of Scotland and France, are such that few men of moderate

fortune can endure the expence of; the poor man must therefore submit to the wealthy. Length of purse will too often
prevail against right and justice. For instance, we are told
by the learned judge [*William*] *Blackstone*, that a question
only on the property of an *ox*, of the value of *three* guineas,
originating under the civil law proceedings in Scotland, after
many interlocutory orders and sentences below, was carried
at length from the court of sessions, the highest court in that
part of Great Britain, by way of *appeal* to the house of lords,
where the question of law and fact was finally determined.
He adds, that no pique or spirit could in the court of king's
bench or common pleas at Westminster, have given continu-
ance to such a cause for a tenth part of the time, nor have
cost a twentieth part of the expence. Yet the costs in the
courts of king's bench and common pleas in England, are in-
finitely greater than those which the people of this country
have ever experienced. We abhor the idea of losing the tran-
scendant privilege of trial by jury, with the loss of which, it
is remarked by the same learned author, that in Sweden,
the liberties of the commons were extinguished by an aristocratic senate: and that *trial by jury* and the liberty of the
people went out together. At the same time we regret the intolerable delay, the enormous expences and infinite vexation
to which the people of this country will be exposed from the
voluminous proceedings of the courts of civil law, and especially from the appellate jurisdiction, by means of which a
man may be drawn from the utmost boundaries of this extensive country to the seat of the supreme court of the nation to contend, perhaps with a wealthy and powerful
adversary. The consequence of this establishment will be an
absolute confirmation of the power of aristocratical influence in the courts of justice; for the common people will not
be able to contend or struggle against it.

Trial by jury in criminal cases may also be excluded by declaring that the libeller for instance shall be liable to an action of debt for a specified sum; thus evading the common law
prosecution by indictment and trial by jury. And the common
course of proceeding against a ship for breach of revenue laws
by information (which will be classed among civil causes) will

at the civil law be within the resort of a court, where no jury intervenes. Besides, the benefit of jury trial, in cases of a criminal nature, which cannot be evaded, will be rendered of little value, by calling the accused to answer far from home; there being no provision that the trial be by a jury of the neighbourhood or country. Thus an inhabitant of Pittsburgh, on a charge of crime committed on the banks of the Ohio, may be obliged to defend himself at the side of the Delaware, and so *vice versa*. To conclude this head: we observe that the judges of the courts of Congress would not be independent, as they are not debarred from holding other offices, during the pleasure of the president and senate, and as they may derive their support in part from fees, alterable by the legislature.

The Constitution Does Not Threaten Trial by Jury

Alexander Hamilton

One of the strongest advocates for centralized government at the Constitutional Convention, Alexander Hamilton became one of the Constitution's staunchest defenders in the ratification debate. Under the pseudonym "Publius," Hamilton and his coauthors, James Madison and John Jay, wrote a series of essays defending the Constitution against attacks by Anti-Federalists. Collectively known as the *Federalist Papers*, these essays are still primary sources for Supreme Court justices seeking to determine the original intent of the Founding Fathers, and they retain their power as monuments of political thought in the Enlightenment. As one of the foremost lawyers in the early republic, Hamilton was outraged at the argument that the Constitution threatened trial by jury, particularly in civil cases. In *Federalist No. 83* he argues that the absence of a constitutional provision for civil juries in no way limits Congress's right to establish such juries. Moreover, he maintains, the limitations on federal jurisdiction ensure that the great majority of civil cases will remain unaffected, allowing state legislatures to continue to set the rules as before. Indeed, given the variety of rules that legislatures have adopted, particularly in civil cases, Hamilton argues that any federal provision would have to be either an ineffective compromise or a roadblock standing in the way of flexibility. Future congresses and legislatures should be free to determine the situations in which civil juries would be useful. Despite Hamilton's reassurances, the issue remained contentious enough that the right to a jury trial in both criminal and civil trials is protected in the Bill of Rights—in the Sixth and Seventh amendments, respectively.

Alexander Hamilton, *Federalist No. 83,* July 5, 9, and 12, 1788.

The objection to the plan of the convention, which has met with most success in this State [New York] is *relative to the want of a constitutional provision* for the trial by jury in civil cases. The disingenuous form in which this objection is usually stated has been repeatedly adverted to and exposed, but continues to be pursued in all the conversations and writings of the opponents of the plan. The mere silence of the Constitution in regard to *civil causes*, is represented as an abolition of the trial by jury, and the declamations to which it has afforded a pretext are artfully calculated to induce a persuasion that this pretended abolition is complete and universal, extending not only to every species of civil, but even to *criminal, causes*. To argue with respect to the latter would be as vain and fruitless as to attempt to demonstrate any of those propositions which, by their own internal evidence, force conviction, when expressed in language adapted to convey their meaning.

With regard to civil causes, subtleties almost too contemptible for refutation have been employed to countenance the surmise that a thing which is only *not provided for*, is entirely *abolished*. Every man of discernment must at once perceive the wide difference between *silence* and *abolition*. But as the inventors of this fallacy have attempted to support it by certain *legal maxims* of interpretation, which they have perverted from their true meaning, it may not be wholly useless to explore the ground they have taken.

False Arguments Refuted

The maxims on which they rely are of this nature: "A specification of particulars is an exclusion of generals"; or, "The expression of one thing is the exclusion of another." Hence, say they, as the Constitution has established the trial by jury in criminal cases, and is silent in respect to civil, this silence is an implied prohibition of trial by jury in regard to the latter.

The rules of legal interpretation are rules of *common-sense*, adopted by the courts in the construction of the laws. The true test, therefore, of a just application of them is its conformity to the source from which they are derived. This being the case, let me ask if it is consistent with common-sense to suppose that a provision obliging the legislative power to commit the trial of criminal causes to juries, is a privation of its right to authorize or permit that mode of trial in other cases? Is it natural to suppose, that a command to do one thing is a prohibition to the doing of another, which there was a previous power to do, and which is not incompatible with the thing commanded to be done? If such a supposition would be unnatural and unreasonable, it cannot be rational to maintain that an injunction of the trial by jury in certain cases is an interdiction of it in others.

A power to constitute courts is a power to prescribe the mode of trial; and consequently, if nothing was said in the Constitution on the subject of juries, the legislature would be at liberty either to adopt that institution or to let it alone. This discretion, in regard to criminal causes, is abridged by an express injunction of trial by jury in all such cases; but it is, of course, left at large in relation to civil causes, there being a total silence on this head. The specification of an obligation to try all criminal causes in a particular mode, excludes indeed the obligation of employing the same mode in civil causes, but does not abridge *the power* of the legislature to appoint that mode if it should be thought proper. The pretence, therefore, that the national legislature would not be at liberty to submit all the civil causes of federal cognizance to the determination of juries, is a pretence destitute of all foundation.

From these observations this conclusion results: that the trial by jury in civil cases would not be abolished; and that the use attempted to be made of the maxims which have been quoted, is contrary to reason, and therefore inadmissible. Even if these maxims had a precise technical sense, corresponding with the idea of those who employ them upon the present occasion, which, however, is not the case, they would still be inapplicable to a constitution of government. In relation to such a subject, the natural and obvious sense of its provisions, apart from any technical rules, is the true criterion of construction.

Limitations on Federal Jurisdictions

Having now seen that the maxims relied upon will not bear the use made of them, let us endeavor to ascertain their proper application. This will be best done by examples. The plan of the convention declares that the power of Congress, or, in other words, of the *national legislature*, shall extend to certain enumerated cases. This specification of particulars evidently excludes all pretension to a general legislative authority, because an affirmative grant of special powers would be absurd, as well as useless, if a general authority was intended.

In like manner the authority of the federal judicatures is declared by the Constitution to comprehend certain cases particularly specified. The expression of those cases marks the precise limits, beyond which the federal courts cannot extend their jurisdiction, because the objects of their cognizance being enumerated, the specification would be nugatory if it did not exclude all ideas of more extensive authority.

These examples are sufficient to elucidate the maxims which have been mentioned, and to designate the manner in which they should be used.

Most Cases Unaffected

From what has been said, it must appear unquestionably true that trial by jury is in no case abolished by the proposed Constitution, and it is equally true, that in those controversies between individuals in which the great body of the people are likely to be interested, that institution will remain precisely in the same situation in which it is placed by the State constitutions. The foundation of this assertion is, that the national judiciary will have no cognizance of them, and of course they will remain determinable as heretofore by the State courts only, and in the manner which the State constitutions and laws prescribe. All land causes, except where claims under the grants of different States come into question, and all other controversies between the citizens of the same State, unless where they depend upon positive violations of the articles of union, by acts of the State legislatures, will belong exclusively to the jurisdiction of the State tribunals. Add to this, that admiralty causes, and almost all those which are of equity jurisdiction, are determinable under our own government without the intervention of a jury, and the inference from the whole will be, that this institution, as it exists with us at present, cannot possibly be affected to any great extent by the proposed alteration in our system of government.

The friends and adversaries of the plan of the convention, if they agree in nothing else, concur at least in the value they set upon the trial by jury; or if there is any difference between them it consists in this: the former regard it as a valuable safeguard to liberty; the latter represent it as the very palladium of free government. For my own part, the more the operation of the institution has fallen under my observation, the more reason I have discovered for holding it in high estimation; and it would be altogether superfluous to examine to what extent it deserves to be esteemed useful or essential in a representative republic, or how much more merit it may be entitled to, as a defence against the oppressions of an hereditary monarch, than as a barrier to the tyranny of popular magistrates in a popular government. Discussions of this kind would be more curious than beneficial, as all are satisfied of the utility of the institution, and of its friendly aspect to liberty. But I must acknowledge that I cannot readily discern the inseparable connection between the existence of liberty, and the trial by jury in civil cases. Arbitrary impeachments, arbitrary methods of prosecuting pretended offences, and arbitrary punishments upon arbitrary convictions, have ever appeared to me the great engines of judicial despotism; and all these have relation to criminal proceedings. The trial by jury in criminal cases, aided by the *habeas-corpus* act, seems therefore to be alone concerned in the question. And both of these are provided for, in the most ample manner, in the plan of the convention. . . .

Juries as a Safeguard Against Corruption

The excellence of the trial by jury in civil cases appears to depend on circumstances foreign to the preservation of liberty. The strongest argument in its favor is, that it is a security against corruption. As there is always more time and better opportunity to tamper with a standing body of magistrates than with a jury summoned for the occasion, there is room to suppose that a corrupt influence would more easily find its way to the former than to the latter. The force of this consideration is, however, diminished by others. The sheriff, who is the summoner of ordinary juries, and the clerks of courts, who have the nomination of special juries, are themselves standing officers, and, acting individually, may be supposed more accessible to the touch of corruption than the judges, who are a collective body. It is not difficult to see, that it would be in the power of those officers to select jurors who would serve the purpose of the party as well as a corrupted bench. In the next place, it may fairly be supposed, that there would be less difficulty in gaining some of the jurors promiscuously taken from the public mass, than in gaining men who had been chosen

Alexander Hamilton

by the government for their probity and good character. But making every deduction for these considerations, the trial by jury must still be a valuable check upon corruption. It greatly multiplies the impediments to its success. As matters now stand, it would be necessary to corrupt both court and jury; for where the jury have gone evidently wrong, the court will generally grant a new trial, and it would be in most cases of little use to practise upon the jury, unless the court could be likewise gained. Here then is a double security; and it will readily be perceived that this complicated agency tends to preserve the purity of both institutions. By increasing the obstacles to success, it discourages attempts to seduce the integrity of either. The temptations to prostitution which the judges might have to surmount, must certainly be much fewer, while the coöperation of a jury is necessary, than they might be, if they had themselves the exclusive determination of all causes.

Notwithstanding, therefore, the doubts I have expressed, as to the essentiality of trial by jury in civil cases to liberty, I admit that it is in most cases, under proper regulations, an excellent method of determining questions of property; and that on this account alone it would be entitled to a constitutional provision in its favor if it were possible to fix with accuracy the limits within which it ought to be comprehended. This is, however, in its own nature an affair of much difficulty; and men not blinded by enthusiasm must be sensible that in a federal government, which is a composition of societies whose ideas and institutions in relation to the matter materially vary from each other, that difficulty must be not a little augmented. For my own part, at every new view I take of the subject, I become more convinced of the reality of the obstacles which, we are authoritatively informed, prevented the insertion of a provision on this head in the plan of the convention. . . .

Mandating Civil Juries Not Possible or Necessary

In short, the more it is considered the more arduous will appear the task of fashioning a provision in such a form as not to express too little to answer the purpose, or too much to be advisable; or which might not have opened other sources of opposition to the great and essential object of introducing a firm national government.

I cannot but persuade myself, on the other hand, that the different lights in which the subject has been placed in the course of these observations, will go far towards removing in candid minds the apprehensions they may have entertained on the point. They have tended to show that the security of liberty is materially concerned only in the trial by jury in criminal cases, which is provided for in the most ample manner in the plan of the convention; that even in far the greatest proportion of civil cases, and those in which the great body of the community is interested, that mode of trial will remain in its full force, as established in the State constitutions, untouched and unaffected by the plan of the convention; that it is in no case abolished by that plan; and that there are great if not insurmountable difficulties in the way of making any precise and proper provision for it in a Constitution for the United States.

Leave It to the Legislatures

The best judges of the matter will be the least anxious for a constitutional establishment of the trial by jury in civil cases, and will be the most ready to admit that the changes which are continually happening in the affairs of society may render a different mode of determining questions of property preferable in many cases in which that mode of trial now prevails. For my part, I acknowledge myself to be convinced that even in this State [New York] it might be advantageously extended to some cases to which it does not at present apply, and might as advantageously be abridged in others. It is conceded by all reasonable men that it ought not to obtain in all cases. The examples of innovations which contract its ancient limits, as well in these States as in Great Britain, afford a strong presumption that its former extent has been found inconvenient, and give room to suppose that future experience may discover the propriety and utility of other exceptions. I suspect it to be impossible in the nature of the thing to fix the salutary point at which the operation of the institution ought to stop, and this is with me a strong argument for leaving the matter to the discretion of the legislature.

This is now clearly understood to be the case in Great Britain, and it is equally so in the State of Connecticut; and yet it may be safely affirmed that more numerous encroachments have been made upon the trial by jury in this State since the Revolution, though provided for by a positive article of our constitution, than has happened in the same time either in Connecticut or Great Britain. It may be added that these encroachments have generally originated with the men who endeavor to persuade the people they are the warmest defenders of popular liberty, but who have rarely suffered constitutional obstacles to arrest them in a favorite career. The truth is that the general GENIUS of a government is all that can be substantially relied upon for permanent effects. Particular provisions, though not altogether useless, have far less virtue and efficacy than are commonly ascribed to them; and the want of them will never be, with men of sound discernment, a decisive objection to any plan which exhibits the leading characters of a good government.

It certainly sounds not a little harsh and extraordinary to affirm that there is no security for liberty in a Constitution which expressly establishes the trial by jury in criminal cases, because it does not do it in civil also; while it is a notorious fact that Connecticut, which has been always regarded as the most popular State in the Union, can boast of no constitutional provision for either.

CHAPTER TWO

The Supreme Court Defines the Right to Trial by Jury

The Bill of Rights

States Must Provide Jury Trials for Serious Crimes

Byron R. White

One of the most important constitutional issues is the question of "incorporation." The Fourteenth Amendment, passed in 1868, declares, "No State shall make or enforce any law which shall abridge the privileges or immunities of citizens of the United States; nor shall any State deprive any person of life, liberty, or property, without due process of law." Since then, the Supreme Court has used this "due process" clause to "incorporate" some of the provisions in the Bill of Rights into state law—that is, the Court has made it illegal for states to pass laws that infringe on some rights protected in the Bill of Rights. The Court has never given a blanket answer to the incorporation question, allowing states flexibility in some areas while denying it in areas it deemed fundamental to American citizenship. In 1968 the Court faced the question of whether trial by jury was one of those fundamental rights. At the time Louisiana required jury trials only in cases where the defendant could be sentenced to death or to hard labor. When Gary Duncan was convicted by a judge of simple battery and sentenced to sixty days in prison and a $150 fine, he appealed on the basis that his right to trial by jury had been denied. The Court found for Duncan, declaring that anyone accused of a "serious crime" in state or federal court had the right to trial by jury. Justice Byron R. White, who served on the Supreme Court from 1962 to 1993, wrote the following opinion for the majority.

Byron R. White, majority opinion, *Duncan v. Louisiana,* 391 U.S. 145, May 20, 1968.

Appellant, Gary Duncan, was convicted of simple battery in the Twenty-fifth Judicial District Court of Louisiana. Under Louisiana law simple battery is a misdemeanor, punishable by a maximum of two years' imprisonment and a $300 fine. Appellant sought trial by jury, but because the Louisiana Constitution grants jury trials only in cases in which capital punishment or imprisonment at hard labor may be imposed, the trial judge denied the request. Appellant was convicted and sentenced to serve 60 days in the parish prison and pay a fine of $150. Appellant sought review in the Supreme Court of Louisiana, asserting that the denial of jury trial violated rights guaranteed to him by the United States Constitution. The Supreme Court, finding "[n]o error of law in the ruling complained of," denied appellant a writ of certiorari. Appellant sought review in this Court, alleging that the Sixth and Fourteenth Amendments to the United States Constitution secure the right to jury trial in state criminal prosecutions where a sentence as long as two years may be imposed. We noted probable jurisdiction, and set the case for oral argument.

Appellant was 19 years of age when tried. While driving on Highway 23 in Plaquemines Parish on October 18, 1966, he saw two younger cousins engaged in a conversation by the side of the road with four white boys. Knowing his cousins, Negroes who had recently transferred to a formerly all-white high school, had reported the occurrence of racial incidents at the school, Duncan stopped the car, got out, and approached the six boys. At trial the white boys and a white onlooker testified, as did appellant and his cousins. The testimony was in dispute on many points, but the witnesses agreed that appellant and the white boys spoke to each other, that appellant encouraged his cousins to break off the encounter and enter his car, and that appellant was about to enter the car himself for the purpose of driving away with his cousins. The whites testified that just before getting in the car appellant slapped Herman Landry, one of the white boys, on the elbow. The Negroes testified that appellant had not slapped Landry, but had merely touched him. The trial judge concluded that the State had proved beyond a reasonable

doubt that Duncan had committed simple battery, and found
him guilty.

Applying the Fourteenth Amendment

The Fourteenth Amendment denies the States the power to
"deprive any person of life, liberty, or property, without due
process of law." In resolving conflicting claims concerning the
meaning of this specious language, the Court has looked increasingly to the Bill of Rights for guidance; many of the rights
guaranteed by the first eight Amendments to the Constitution
have been held to be protected against state action by the Due
Process Clause of the Fourteenth Amendment. That clause
now protects the right to compensation for property taken by
the State; the rights of speech, press, and religion covered the
First Amendment; the Fourth Amendment rights to be free
from unreasonable searches and seizures and to have excluded
from criminal trials any evidence illegally seized; the right
guaranteed by the Fifth Amendment to be free of compelled
self-incrimination; and the Sixth Amendment rights to counsel, to a speedy and public trial, to confrontation of opposing
witnesses, and to compulsory process for obtaining witnesses.

The test for determining whether a right extended by the
Fifth and Sixth Amendments with respect to federal criminal
proceedings is also protected against state action by the Fourteenth Amendment has been phrased in a variety of ways in
the opinions of this Court. The question has been asked
whether a right is among those "fundamental principles of
liberty and justice which lie at the base of all our civil and political institutions," *Powell v. Alabama* (1932); whether it is
"basic in our system of jurisprudence," *In re Oliver* (1948); and
whether it is "a fundamental right, essential to a fair trial,"
Gideon v. Wainwright (1963); *Malloy v. Hogan* (1964); *Pointer
v. Texas* (1965). The claim before us is that the right to trial
by jury guaranteed by the Sixth Amendment meets these
tests. The position of Louisiana, on the other hand, is that the
Constitution imposes upon the States no duty to give a jury
trial in any criminal case, regardless of the seriousness of the
crime or the size of the punishment which may be imposed.
Because we believe that trial by jury in criminal cases is fun-

damental to the American scheme of justice, we hold that the Fourteenth Amendment guarantees a right of jury trial in all criminal cases which—were they to be tried in a federal court—would come within the Sixth Amendment's guarantee. Since we consider the appeal before us to be such a case, we hold that the Constitution was violated when appellant's demand for jury trial was refused.

Trial by Jury Long Established

The history of trial by jury in criminal cases has been frequently told. It is sufficient for present purposes to say that by the time our Constitution was written, jury trial in criminal cases had been in existence in England for several centuries and carried impressive credentials traced by many to Magna Carta. Its preservation and proper operation as a protection against arbitrary rule were among the major objectives of the revolutionary settlement which was expressed in the Declaration and Bill of Rights of 1689. In the 18th century [jurist William] Blackstone could write:

> Our law has therefore wisely placed this strong and two-fold barrier, of a presentment and a trial by jury, between the liberties of the people and the prerogative of the crown. It was necessary, for preserving the admirable balance of our constitution, to vest the executive power of the laws in the prince: and yet this power might be dangerous and destructive to that very constitution, if exerted without check or control, by justices of over and terminer occasionally named by the crown; who might then, as in France or Turkey, imprison, dispatch, or exile any man that was obnoxious to the government, by an instant declaration that such is their will and pleasure. But the founders of the English law have, with excellent forecast, contrived that . . . the truth of every accusation, whether preferred in the shape of indictment, information, or appeal, should afterwards be confirmed by the unanimous suffrage of twelve of his equals and neighbours, indifferently chosen and superior to all suspicion.

Jury trial came to America with English colonists, and received strong support from them. Royal interference with the jury trial was deeply resented. Among the resolutions adopted by the First Congress of the American Colonies (the Stamp Act Congress) on October 19, 1765—resolutions deemed by their authors to state "the most essential rights and liberties of the colonists"—was the declaration: "That trial by jury is the inherent and invaluable right of every British subject in these colonies."

The First Continental Congress, in the resolve of October 14, 1774, objected to trials before judges dependent upon the Crown alone for their salaries and to trials in England for alleged crimes committed in the colonies; the Congress therefore declared: "That the respective colonies are entitled to the common law of England, and more especially to the great and inestimable privilege of being tried by their peers of the vicinage, according to the course of that law."

Right to Jury Trial Fundamental in U.S. History

The Declaration of Independence stated solemn objections to the King's making "Judges dependent on his Will alone, for the tenure of their offices, and the amount and payment of their salaries," to his "depriving us in many cases, of the benefits of Trial by Jury," and to his "transporting us beyond Seas to be tried for pretended offenses." The Constitution itself, in Art. III, commanded: "The Trial of all Crimes, except in Cases of Impeachment, shall be by Jury; and such Trial shall be held in the State where the said Crimes shall have been committed." Objections to the Constitution because of the absence of a bill of rights were met by the immediate submission and adoption of the Bill of Rights. Included was the Sixth Amendment which, among other things, provided: "In all criminal prosecutions, the accused shall enjoy the right to a speedy and public trial, by an impartial jury of the State and district wherein the crime shall have been committed." The constitutions adopted by the original States guaranteed jury trial. Also, the constitution of every State entering the Union thereafter in one form or another protected the right to jury trial in criminal cases.

Even such skeletal history is impressive support for considering the right to jury trial in criminal cases to be fundamental to our system of justice, an importance frequently recognized in the opinions of this Court. For example, the Court has said [in *Thompson v. Utah* (1968)]: "Those who emigrated to this country from England brought with them this great privilege 'as their birthright and inheritance, as a part of that admirable common law which had fenced around and interposed barriers on every side against the approaches of arbitrary power.'"

Jury trial continues to receive strong support. The laws of every State guarantee a right to jury trial in serious criminal cases; no State has dispensed with it; nor are there significant movements underway to do so. Indeed, the three most recent state constitutional revisions, in Maryland, Michigan, and New York, carefully preserved the right of the accused to have the judgment of a jury when tried for a serious crime.

Answering Objections

We are aware of prior cases in this Court in which the prevailing opinion contains statements contrary to our holding today that the right to jury trial in serious criminal cases is a fundamental right and hence must be recognized by the States as part of their obligation to extend due process of law to all persons within their jurisdiction. Louisiana relies especially on *Maxwell v. Dow* (1900); *Palko v. Connecticut* (1937); and *Snyder v. Massachusetts* (1934). None of these cases, however, dealt with a State which had purported to dispense entirely with a jury trial in serious criminal cases. *Maxwell* held that no provision of the Bill of Rights applied to the States—a position long since repudiated—and that the Due Process Clause of the Fourteenth Amendment did not prevent a State from trying a defendant for a noncapital offense with fewer than 12 men on the jury. It did not deal with a case in which no jury at all had been provided. In neither *Palko* nor *Snyder* was jury trial actually at issue, although both cases contain important dicta asserting that the right to jury trial is not essential to ordered liberty and may be dispensed with by the States regardless of the Sixth and Fourteenth Amendments.

These observations, though weighty and respectable, are nevertheless dicta, unsupported by holdings in this Court that a State may refuse a defendant's demand for a jury trial when he is charged with a serious crime. Perhaps because the right to jury trial was not directly at stake, the Court's remarks about the jury in *Palko* and *Snyder* took no note of past or current developments regarding jury trials, did not consider its purposes and functions, attempted no inquiry into how well it was performing its job, and did not discuss possible distinctions between civil and criminal cases. In *Malloy v. Hogan*, the Court rejected *Palko*'s discussion of the self-incrimination clause. Respectfully, we reject the prior dicta regarding jury trial in criminal cases.

The guarantees of jury trial in the Federal and State Constitutions reflect a profound judgment about the way in which law should be enforced and justice administered. A right to jury trial is granted to criminal defendants in order to prevent oppression by the Government. Those who wrote our constitutions knew from history and experience that it was necessary to protect against unfounded criminal charges brought to eliminate enemies and against judges too responsive to the voice of higher authority. The framers of the constitutions strove to create an independent judiciary but insisted upon further protection against arbitrary action. Providing an accused with the right to be tried by a jury of his peers gave him an inestimable safeguard against the corrupt or overzealous prosecutor and against the compliant, biased, or eccentric judge. If the defendant preferred the common-sense judgment of a jury to the more tutored but perhaps less sympathetic reaction of the single judge, he was to have it. Beyond this, the jury trial provisions in the Federal and State Constitutions reflect a fundamental decision about the exercise of official power—a reluctance to entrust plenary powers over the life and liberty of the citizen to one judge or to a group of judges. Fear of unchecked power, so typical of our State and Federal Governments in other respects, found expression in the criminal law in this insistence upon community participation in the determination of guilt or innocence. The deep commitment of the Nation to the right of jury trial in serious criminal cases as a defense against arbitrary law enforcement qualifies for protection under the Due Process Clause of the Fourteenth Amendment, and must therefore be respected by the States. . . .

The State of Louisiana urges that holding that the Fourteenth Amendment assures a right to jury trial will cast doubt on the integrity of every trial conducted without a jury. Plainly, this is not the import of our holding. Our conclusion is that in the American States, as in the federal judicial system, a general grant of jury trial for serious offenses is a fundamental right, essential for preventing miscarriages of justice and for assuring that fair trials are provided for all defendants. We would not assert, however, that every criminal trial—or any particular trial—held before a judge alone is unfair or that a defendant may never be as fairly treated by a judge as he would be by a jury. Thus we hold no constitutional doubts about the practices, common in both federal and state courts, of accepting waivers of jury trial and prosecuting petty crimes without extending a right to jury trial. However, the fact is that in most places more trials for serious crimes are to juries than to a court alone; a great many defendants prefer the judgment of a jury to that of a court. Even where defendants are satisfied with bench trials, the right to a jury trial very likely serves its intended purpose of making judicial or prosecutorial unfairness less likely.

Serious Crimes Require Jury Trials

Louisiana's final contention is that even if it must grant jury trials in serious criminal cases, the conviction before us is valid and constitutional because here the petitioner was tried for simple battery and was sentenced to only 60 days in the parish prison. We are not persuaded. It is doubtless true that there is a category of petty crimes or offenses which is not subject to the Sixth Amendment jury trial provision and should not be subject to the Fourteenth Amendment jury trial requirement here applied to the States. Crimes carrying possible penalties up to six months do not require a jury trial if they otherwise qualify as petty offenses, *Cheff v. Schnackenberg* (1966). But the penalty authorized for a particular crime is of major relevance in determining whether it is serious or not and may in itself, if severe enough, subject the trial to the mandates of the Sixth Amendment. *District of Columbia v. Clawans* (1937). The penalty authorized by the law of the locality may be taken "as a gauge of its social and ethical judgments," of the crime in question. In *Clawans* the defendant was jailed for 60 days, but it was the 90-day authorized punishment on which the Court focused in determining that the offense was not one for which the Constitution assured trial by jury. In the case before us the Legislature of Louisiana has made simple battery a criminal offense punishable by imprisonment for up to two years and a fine. The question, then, is whether a crime carrying such a penalty is an offense which Louisiana may insist on trying without a jury.

We think not. So-called petty offenses were tried without juries both in England and in the Colonies and have always been held to be exempt from the otherwise comprehensive language of the Sixth Amendment's jury trial provisions. There is no substantial evidence that the Framers intended to depart from this established common-law practice, and the possible consequences to defendants from convictions for petty offenses have been thought insufficient to outweigh the benefits to efficient law enforcement and simplified judicial administration resulting from the availability of speedy and inexpensive nonjury adjudications. These same considerations compel the same result under the Fourteenth Amendment. Of course the boundaries of the petty offense category have always been ill-defined, if not ambulatory. In the absence of an explicit constitutional provision, the definitional task necessarily falls on the courts, which must either pass upon the validity of legislative attempts to identify those petty offenses which are exempt from jury trial or, where the legislature has not addressed itself to the problem, themselves face the question in the first instance. In either case it is necessary to draw a line in the spectrum of crime, separating petty from serious infractions. This process, although essential, cannot be wholly satisfactory, for it requires attaching different consequences to events which, when they lie near the line, actually differ very little.

In determining whether the length of the authorized prison term or the seriousness of other punishment is enough in itself to require a jury trial, we are counseled by *District of Columbia v. Clawans*, to refer to objective criteria, chiefly the existing laws and practices in the Nation. In the federal system, petty offenses are defined as those punishable by no more than six months in prison and a $500 fine. In 49 of the 50 States crimes subject to trial without a jury, which occasionally include simple battery, are punishable by no more than one year in jail. Moreover, in the late 18th century in America crimes triable without a jury were for the most part punishable by no more than a six-month prison term, although there appear to have been exceptions to this rule. We need not, however, settle in this case the exact location of the line between petty offenses and serious crimes. It is sufficient for our purposes to hold that a crime punishable by two years in prison is, based on past and contemporary standards in this country, a serious crime and not a petty offense. Consequently, appellant was entitled to a jury trial and it was error to deny it.

The judgment below is reversed and the case is remanded for proceedings not inconsistent with this opinion.

The Supreme Court Allows Smaller Juries

Randolph N. Jonakait

Having declared trial by jury a fundamental right in *Duncan v. Louisiana*, the Supreme Court began to take a closer look at some of the particular judicial rules that differed from state to state, such as jury size. In *Williams v. Florida*, the Court found that the traditional twelve-person jury was not in fact a legal necessity; a six-person jury, but no smaller, would pass constitutional muster. As Randolph N. Jonakait, a professor of law at New York Law School, explains, this finding overturned a previous ruling, in *Thompson v. Utah*, holding that citizens were entitled to a common law jury of twelve members, at least in federal court. Drawing on a number of studies, as well as his own experience as a lawyer for the New York City Legal Aid Society, Jonakait disputes the Court's finding that size is not especially significant to jury fairness. For Jonakait, twelve-person juries are fairer, more likely to contain minority members, and less inconsistent than smaller juries.

In 1968 *Duncan v. Louisiana* held that the right to a jury trial in a criminal case is fundamental and that the same right applies in both state and federal prosecutions. The federal courts had but a single model for a jury trial. A jury consisted of twelve people who had to reach unanimity in order to render a verdict, as the Supreme Court had said two year earlier. The right applied to trials of any federal crime that was not "petty," which was defined as a crime carrying a possible penalty of more than six months.

Randolph N. Jonakait, *The American Jury System*. New Haven, CT: Yale University Press, 2003. Copyright © 2003 by Yale University. All rights reserved. Reproduced by permission.

The states, in contrast, had diverse models for juries. Some states employed juries smaller than twelve; some did not require juries to be unanimous in their decisions; and although all states guaranteed jury trials, they varied concerning the kinds of crimes to which this right applied. Indeed, Louisiana law at the time of *Duncan* illustrated all these complexities. Jury trials were guaranteed, but only for crimes that carried sentences of death or hard labor. If not, the trial went to a judge without a jury. If the crime permitted, but did not require, a sentence of hard labor, the accused was entitled to a five-person jury with a unanimous verdict. If the crime required a punishment of hard labor, a twelve-person jury was required, but only nine of the jurors had to agree to reach a verdict. If the crime was punishable by death, the jury was twelve and the verdict had to be unanimous.

After *Duncan*, the Supreme Court began to consider whether the different state forms of jury trials were constitutional. The process began in 1970 when the Court in *Williams v. Florida* held that a jury of six passed constitutional muster. In doing so, the Court abandoned its precedent of *Thompson v. Utah*, set at the end of the nineteenth century.

Thompson v. Utah

A Mr. Thompson was charged in the Utah territory with calf-rustling. He was tried and convicted in the territorial courts by a jury of twelve, as federal law dictated, but his motion for a new trial was granted. This second trial was held in the state court because by then Utah had gained statehood. As the Utah constitution permitted, this jury had only eight people. In 1898 the case made its way to the Supreme Court, which first noted that the Sixth Amendment right to a jury trial applied in the territorial courts and that, whatever the normal powers of the state, any trial for a crime committed before statehood had to provide a jury consistent with the federal constitution. The Court stated that the federal jury trial right required a jury constituted as it was in the common law of this country and England. This, *Thompson* concluded, was a jury of twelve acting unanimously. "The wise men who framed the constitution of the United States and the people who approved it were of the opinion that life and liberty, when involved in criminal prosecutions, would not be adequately secured except through the unanimous verdict of twelve jurors. It was not for the state, in respect of a crime committed within its limits while it was a territory, to dispense with that guaranty simply because its people had reached the conclusion that the truth could be as well ascertained, and the liberty of an accused be as well guarded, by eight as well as by twelve jurors in a criminal case."

Williams v. Florida

Seventy years later the Supreme Court again considered the issue of jury size. This Court found that *Thompson*'s basic approach was wrong. *Williams v. Florida* agreed that the common law required juries of twelve, but the Court went on to state that "there is absolutely no indication in 'the intent of the Framers' of an explicit decision to equate the constitutional and common-law characteristics of the jury." Instead, the Court concluded that no one could now know precisely what the framers meant by a jury trial.

Rather than searching history for the constitutionally required number of jurors, *Williams* concluded that a jury's characteristics should be defined by the function that the framers envisioned for juries: the prevention of governmental oppression. *Williams* continued, "Given this purpose, the essential feature of a jury obviously lies in the interposition between the accused and his accuser of the commonsense judgment of a group of laymen, and in the community participation and shared responsibility that results from the group's determination of guilt or innocence." Differently sized bodies could serve these functions, but "the number should probably be large enough to promote group deliberation, free from outside attempts at intimidation, and to provide a fair possibility for obtaining a representative cross-section of the community."

The Court, citing but a few experiments and mostly using its own instincts, concluded that juries of six would little affect how well juries performed. The Court intuited that the change in community representation between juries of six and twelve "seems likely to be negligible," and while juries of six might be less likely to hang than juries of twelve, this "seems unlikely to inure perceptibly to the advantage of either side. . . . And, certainly the reliability of the jury as a factfinder hardly seems likely to be a function of its size." The Court concluded that the twelve-person jury was merely "a historical accident." A jury of six, the Court held, is constitutional.

Studies of Jury Size

Williams engendered a storm of controversy by concluding that halving the historical jury would not affect group deliberations and community participation. Scholars quickly produced a flurry of studies about how size affects jury performance. Three years after *Williams*, however, that research did little to alter the Supreme Court's view of smaller juries. In 1973 *Colgrove v. Battin* held that six-person civil juries did not violate the Seventh Amendment's right to juries in civil cases. Consigning its discussion of the studies to a footnote, the Court noted that since 1970, "much has been written about the six-member jury, but nothing that persuades us to depart from the conclusion reached in *Williams*."

In 1978, however, while reviewing Claude Ballew's misdemeanor obscenity conviction by an Atlanta jury of five, the Court took more note of the scholarship regarding jury numbers. The Court now stressed that social science studies showed smaller juries had a negative effect on deliberations. "The smaller the group, the less likely are members to make critical contributions necessary for the solution of a given problem. . . . Memory is important for accurate jury determinations. As juries decrease in size, . . . they are less likely to have members who remember each of the important pieces of evidence or argument. Furthermore, the smaller the group, the less likely it is to overcome the biases of its members to obtain an accurate result. When individual and group decision-making were compared, it was seen that groups performed better because prejudices of individuals were frequently counterbalanced, and objectivity resulted."

These studies also showed that accuracy decreased and inconsistency increased with smaller panels. Moreover, because juries generally hang because one or two jurors hold out against the remainder favoring conviction, the decrease in hung juries resulting from a smaller jury size disproportionately harms criminal defendants by increasing the conviction rate. Finally, the Court noted, smaller juries will not represent the community as well as larger ones. "If a minority viewpoint is shared by 10% of the community, 28.2% of 12-member juries may be expected to have no minority representation, but 53.1% of 6-member juries would have none."

Although these data suggested that the assumptions underlying the acceptance of six-person juries were wrong, the Court did not overturn its earlier decision. Instead, without "pretend[ing] to discern a clear line between six members and five," the Court reaffirmed that six-person juries were constitutional but held that juries of less than six were not.

Research on how size affects jury performance has continued. The studies consistently show that larger juries are more likely to contain minority members, recall more of the evidence, spend more time deliberating, and bring more informational resources to those deliberations than are six-person juries. Just as individuals render more variable decisions than groups, juries of six produce more variability than do juries of twelve. In civil cases, studies generally agree, smaller juries show an increased variability in damages, with a higher average award. . . .

The Supreme Court's Faulty Intuition

Juries can be, and in some places are, smaller than six. In concluding that halving the traditional jury would not significantly affect how juries perform, the Supreme Court cited only a few empirical studies without probing their validity. Instead, it relied almost entirely on its own instincts. Competent studies, however, show these judicial assumptions to be wrong. In other words, the justices did not know what they were talking about.

This may be surprising, but it should not be. Few Supreme Court judges have had much contact with juries. The bar, like almost any human institution, has its own hierarchy. As a general rule, the less a lawyer deals with "common people," the more prestigious the position she holds. The lawyer involved with mergers and acquisitions stands on a higher rung than one dealing with personal injuries or crimes. Supreme Court justices do not represent a cross-section of the bar. They generally come from the bar's elite, and this gentry seldom has much experience with juries. Because the Supreme Court's intuitions about juries do not come from any depth of experience, they should not automatically be trusted.

There is, of course, a broader point here. Supreme Court Justices are educated and thoughtful. If this group's intuitions about juries should be viewed skeptically, surely suspicion is also in order for the views of many others about the jury system, no matter how smart, prestigious, or knowledgeable, when those opinions are based only on intuitions, assertions, and anecdotes and not on extensive experience or serious study.

The Supreme Court Allows Majority Verdicts in State Trials

Jeffrey Abramson

For centuries it was taken for granted that the unanimous verdict was an integral part of the trial by jury, a necessary corollary to proving a case beyond any reasonable doubt. However, this requirement is not the law of the land. Since 1972 the Supreme Court has allowed state, though not federal, juries to convict defendants by a majority vote. That year, as Jeffrey Abramson, a professor of politics at Brandeis University and a former assistant district attorney, explains, the Court broke its long silence on the issue and handed down two decisions allowing for majority verdicts. In the first, *Apodaca v. Oregon*, the defendants claimed that allowing a jury to convict over the objections of minority jurors violated their right to be tried by a true cross-section of the community. In the second, *Johnson v. Louisiana*, the defendant claimed that the majority verdict violated the prosecution's obligation to prove its case beyond a reasonable doubt. As Abramson shows, these arguments impressed such legendary justices as William O. Douglas and Thurgood Marshall. Nevertheless, by 5-4 decisions, the Court ruled against the defendants, and states are now clearly allowed to permit majority verdicts and thus minimize the chance of a hung jury.

For over six hundred years, the unanimous verdict has stood as a distinctive and defining feature of jury trials.

Jeffrey Abramson, *We, the Jury: The Jury System and the Ideal of Democracy*. New York: BasicBooks, 1994. Copyright © 1994 by BasicBooks. Reproduced by permission of HarperCollins Publishers, Inc.

The first recorded instance of a unanimous verdict occurred in 1367, when an English Court refused to accept an 11-1 guilty vote after the lone holdout stated he would rather die in prison than consent to convict. Steadily afterward, the requirement of unanimity took hold. As legal historians Frederick Pollock and Frederic Maitland point out, "From the moment when our records begin, we seem to see a strong desire for unanimity. In a thousand cases the jury is put before us as speaking with a single voice, while any traces of dissent . . . confessed by some only of the jurors are very rare."

Some American colonies briefly authorized majority verdicts in the seventeenth century, apparently because of unfamiliarity with common-law procedures. But by the eighteenth century, it was agreed that verdicts had to be unanimous. Indeed, prior to 1972, no case explicitly disputing the unanimity requirement in criminal cases ever came before the Supreme Court. Incidental references to the "obvious" requirement that criminal jury verdicts be unanimous date to the late 1800s. As the Court noted in 1898, "The wise men who framed the Constitution of the United States and the people who approved it were of [the] opinion that life and liberty, when involved in criminal prosecutions, would not be adequately secured except through the unanimous verdict of twelve jurors." In 1897, a case challenging the necessity of unanimous verdicts in civil cases reached the Court. But the Court readily dismissed the challenge, saying that "no authorities are needed to sustain [the] proposition" that "unanimity was one of the peculiar and essential features of trial by jury at the common law."

Unquestioned acceptance of the concept of unanimous verdict abruptly came to an end, for the criminal jury, in the late 1960s and early 1970s. In 1967, England authorized criminal juries to return verdicts by a margin as low as 10 to 2, so long as the jury deliberated at least two hours. In 1972, in cases from Oregon and Louisiana, the Supreme Court ruled that the Constitution permits state, though not federal, criminal juries to split by a 10-2 or 9-3 margin in noncapital cases. . . .

The 1972 Decisions: Authorizing Nonunanimous Verdicts

Advocates of the unanimous verdict rule presented the Court with two constitutional reasons to mandate unanimity in state criminal jury trials. In *Apodaca v. Oregon*, the defendants argued that unanimity was essential to enforcement of their Sixth Amendment right to be tried before cross-sectional juries. Only the unanimous verdict rule could guarantee effective representation to minority views; anything less empowered majorities simply to outvote minorities.

In *Johnson v. Louisiana*, the defendant was tried before the Supreme Court had extended the Sixth Amendment to state criminal trials. But Johnson argued that Louisiana's acceptance of a 9-3 jury verdict in his case violated his due process rights under the Fourteenth Amendment to have his guilt proved beyond a reasonable doubt. By definition, no jury could reasonably find a defendant's guilt proved beyond a reasonable doubt, he argued, when some of its members continued to harbor doubts.

By a narrow 5-4 margin, the Court rejected both arguments for constitutionalizing the unanimous verdict.

Apodaca v. Oregon: Unanimity and Representation

To decide the Oregon case, the Court first turned to the history of the Sixth Amendment's passage for evidence of what the drafters of the amendment intended to include within the mandatory features of a jury trial. The Court noted that, as originally introduced by James Madison, the proposed amendment provided for trial "by an impartial jury . . . with the requisite of unanimity for conviction, . . . and other accustomed requisites." But the amendment as finally adopted dropped all references to unanimity and "other accustomed requisites." From this legislative history, the Court thought it possible to "draw conflicting inferences." It is possible that Congress simply thought it unnecessary to specify features as customary as unanimity because it was "thought already to be implicit in the very concept of jury." Or perhaps Congress deleted all references to accepted features of the jury in 1791 because it wished to leave specification of the jury's nature for the future.

Because history alone could not resolve the meaning of the Sixth Amendment, the Court approached its decision from a "functional" point of view. Was the requirement of unanimous verdicts so indispensable to the jury's essential functions that it must be considered part of what the Sixth Amendment means by a "jury"? Here, five justices concluded that, for all its longevity, unanimity lacked fundamental importance and thus constitutional stature.

The chief function of the criminal jury, the Court noted, was "to prevent oppression by the Government." To provide this safeguard, the jury places between the accused and the state "the commonsense judgment of a group of laymen . . . representative of a cross section of the community." In terms of this shielding function, five justices could "perceive no difference between juries required to act unanimously and those permitted to convict or acquit by votes of 10 to two or 11 to one."

The Case for Unanimity

On what basis did the Court conclude that unanimity was superfluous to the jury's core functions? The defendants in *Apodaca* characterized the unanimous verdict requirement as a "necessary precondition for the effective application of the cross-section requirement." They reviewed the Court's commitment in other cases to making the jury a representative body. That commitment had led to sweeping reforms to end the systematic exclusion of certain groups from jury panels and to the new requirement for drawing jurors randomly from a cross section of the community. But all these reforms of jury selection would be meaningless, the defendants argued, if unanimity were abandoned, leaving majorities free to ignore and outvote minorities on the jury. As the defendants' brief put it:

> While members of racial, religious, or ethnic minorities, women, poor people, young people or other previously excluded groups may now be represented on

juries, a rule permitting a less than unanimous verdict makes it possible for a verdict to be rendered without their acquiescence and indeed without the consideration of their views.

An amicus brief filed by the American Civil Liberties Union took a similar tack in warning that less than unanimous verdicts make it "easier—perhaps commonplace—for a jury to ignore the viewpoints of minority group members."

These arguments convinced four justices of the Court that unanimous verdicts were vital to the jury's ability to grant effective representation to minority viewpoints. Justice Potter Stewart hypothesized a worst-case scenario where the jury splits along racial lines to convict a defendant "conspicuously identified" as of the same race as the dissenting jurors. Such verdicts contradict the very purposes of recruiting jurors from a cross section of the community, Justice Stewart concluded. They corrode the community's confidence in criminal justice because they let jury verdicts follow racial or class divisions on the jury.

Justice Stewart was frank in conceding that his defense of unanimity rested on a less than rosy picture of the virtues of individual jurors. Ideally, jurors should be virtuous enough to deliberate rationally across group lines, but it takes the unanimous verdict requirement to enforce the ideal. "It does not denigrate the system of trial by jury to acknowledge that it is imperfect, . . . [that there are] serious risks of jury misbehavior, . . . [that juries] sometimes act out of passion and prejudice," Stewart wrote. Human behavior is such that the requirement of unanimity is a necessary "and effective method endorsed by centuries of experience and history to combat the injuries to the fair administration of justice that can be inflicted by community passion and prejudice."

The Court Decides Against Unanimity Requirement

On the other side of the issue, five justices rejected the need for unanimous verdicts by portraying jury behavior in a far more idealized light. With or without the unanimous verdict requirement, jurors retained the duty to deliberate and debate opposing points of view. Technically, of course, Oregon's system would permit jurors to dispense with deliberation altogether if the required majority of ten were present from the beginning. (The dissenters were particularly troubled by the decision of Apodaca's jury to terminate deliberation after only forty-one minutes and return a conviction by a 10-2 vote.)

But five justices found no grounds for believing that a majority of jurors would suddenly cease to live up to the ideal of rational deliberation with the minority, once the unanimity requirement was lifted. Each individual seated on a jury had survived challenges for cause and been found capable of impartial, color-blind, ethnic-blind justice. Lacking evidence to the contrary, the Court would not "assume that the majority of the jury will refuse to weigh the evidence and reach a decision upon rational grounds, just as it must now do in order to obtain unanimous verdicts, or that a majority will deprive a man of his liberty on the basis of prejudice when a minority is presenting a reasonable argument in favor of acquittal." It may be that the minority viewpoint is outvoted in the end. But this was no evidence that the majority had cast its votes "based on prejudice rather than the evidence." In short, according to the Court, there was no reason to think minority views were not being heard, discussed, and therefore adequately represented under Oregon's 10-2 verdict rule.

Johnson v. Louisiana: The Problem of Doubt

Under the due process clause of the Fourteenth Amendment, it had previously been settled that the Constitution required states to prove a defendant's guilt beyond a reasonable doubt. In the Louisiana case, Johnson argued that the remaining, unresolved doubts of three of his jurors meant that the reasonable doubt standard had not been met at his trial.

A majority of the Court found no inconsistency between nonunanimous verdicts and proof beyond a reasonable doubt. To begin with, the Court pointed out the unquestioned practice of permitting defendants to be retried, when a jury hung and failed to agree on guilt. If Johnson were correct that the doubts of some jurors equaled a failure of proof beyond a reasonable doubt, then the proper remedy for a hung jury would be acquittal, not a second trial.

Proof beyond a reasonable doubt, the Court agreed, was meant to underwrite the accuracy and reliability of jury verdicts. But rational persons may disagree in their judgments. Nine persons can conscientiously and in good faith follow their instructions to be convinced beyond a reasonable doubt, even in the face of the doubts of three of their colleagues. All that is required is that the majority listen to the arguments for acquittal, terminating deliberation and "outvot[ing] a minority only after reasoned discussion has ceased to have persuasive effect or to serve any other purpose—when a minority, that is, continues to insist upon acquittal without having persuasive reasons in support of its position."

As in *Apodaca*, the Court presumed that jurors would behave according to this deliberative ideal. Indeed, if any jurors were being irrational, it was more likely to be those few who persevered in their doubts when a majority of the jury, after having considered the dissenters' views, remained convinced of guilt or innocence. The Court suggested that these dissenting jurors should be the ones asking whether their views were reasonable, when argument failed to persuade such a majority of the jury. Here the Court alluded to *Allen v. United States*, the so-called dynamite charge case authorizing judges to instruct deadlocked juries that "if much the larger number were for conviction, a dissenting juror should consider whether his doubt was a reasonable one which made no impression upon the minds of so many men, equally honest, equally intelligent with himself."

The *Allen* charge is often criticized for suggesting to jurors that they compromise simply to avoid hanging. In his concurring opinion, Justice Lewis Powell took the unanimous verdict to task on precisely this ground. For Powell, the unanimity rule put pressure on jurors to compromise, "despite the frequent absence of a rational basis for such compromise." In the end, so-called unanimity led "not to full agreement among the 12 but to agreement by none and compromise by all." This meant that greater accuracy might be achieved under a system that permitted nine jurors, convinced that guilt has or has not been proved beyond a reasonable doubt, to deliver the verdict without having to compromise with a few holdouts who resist rational argument.

A Question of Appearance

Justice Powell made the strongest argument against unanimity by separating it from the goal of reaching truth. But what if a compromise verdict agreed to by all jurors leads to greater popular *belief* that justice has been done? . . . This legitimizing function, the Court stressed, was one of the main reasons for placing justice in the hands of laypersons. It seems plausible to assume that a community will have greater confidence that justice has been done when these laypersons agree on the verdict. It seems especially apparent that a minority section of the community would suspect verdicts rendered over the objections of the only minority members on the panel. Thus, what Justice Powell harshly criticized as the "irrational" compromises wrought by unanimity may unfairly denigrate unanimity's important role in legitimizing verdicts in the public eye.

Of course, Justice Powell was suggesting that the public was wrong to assume a connection between unanimous verdicts and accurate verdicts. But there can be little doubt that for centuries the unanimous verdict has inspired confidence in the administration of justice. As political scientist Gary Jacobsohn points out, to jettison unanimity and ask the public to accept majority verdicts as equally reliable could well sap the legitimacy of the system. Even Justice Powell accepted this historic, symbolic connection between the unanimity of jury verdicts and their legitimacy when he favored preserving the time-honored tradition of unanimous verdicts in federal trials.

Dissenters Suspect Court's Decision Undermines Reasonable Doubt Standard

In dissent, Justices William Douglas and Thurgood Marshall emphatically endorsed the logical connection between unanimity and proof beyond a reasonable doubt. For Justice Marshall, the "doubts of a single juror [were] . . . evidence that the government has failed to carry its burden" of proof. This was so because no juror's doubts could ever be dismissed as a sign of "irrationality." Assuming the juror is mentally competent, the "'irrationality' that enters into the deliberation process is precisely the essence of the right to a jury trial." Each juror was there to be "a spokesman . . . simply for himself." For Marshall, unanimity was the only method for empowering the solitary dissenting voice when it came to the question of whether reasonable doubt existed.

Likewise for Justice Douglas, under unanimous verdict conditions proof beyond a reasonable doubt sponsored a long and intense process of deliberation where each juror seriously wrestled with the doubts of others. Under majority verdict conditions, deliberation could be cut off before the dissenters had full opportunity to argue for their doubts. Douglas conceded that, even after they had the vote, the majority might deign to listen to the doubts of the minority. But there was all the difference in the world between deliberation entered into as "courtesy dialogue" or "polite and academic conversation" and deliberation entered into because of a necessity to convince others. In the former case, deliberation was reduced to a weak matter of "majority grace," in Justice William Brennan's term. In the latter case, deliberation aided the search for truth by privileging arguments strong enough to win the consent of all. Proof beyond a reasonable doubt was met only when deliberation, in this stronger form, harmonized the views of all jurors.

Peremptory Challenges Cannot Be Used to Create a Racially Stacked Jury

Lewis Powell

Traditionally, both prosecutors and defense attorneys are allowed to challenge jurors during voir dire, the jury selection process. In addition to challenges for cause, such as a personal bias for or against the defendant, each side usually has a number of peremptory challenges, allowing it to dismiss potential jurors from the jury pool (called the "venire") for unstated reasons. In *Batson v. Kentucky*, the Supreme Court set an important limit to peremptory challenges. The prosecutor in the case had used peremptory challenges to remove all the eligible blacks from the jury pool, with the result that an all-white jury convicted Batson, a black man, of burglary. Batson appealed on the grounds that he had been denied equal protection, and the Court agreed. Writing for the majority, Justice Lewis Powell (who served on the Court from 1972 to 1987) explains that peremptory challenges cannot be used to circumvent the equal protection clause, which guarantees African Americans the right to serve on juries. In addition to threatening the rights of the accused, Powell notes, racial discrimination in jury selection undermines public confidence in the justice system, harming the entire community.

In *Swain v. Alabama*, this Court recognized that a "State's purposeful or deliberate denial to Negroes on account of race of participation as jurors in the administration of justice

Lewis Powell, majority opinion, *Batson v. Kentucky,* 475 U.S. 79, April 30, 1986.

violates the Equal Protection Clause." This principle has been "consistently and repeatedly" reaffirmed in numerous decisions of this Court both preceding and following *Swain*. We reaffirm the principle today.

More than a century ago, the Court decided that the State denies a black defendant equal protection of the laws when it puts him on trial before a jury from which members of his race have been purposefully excluded. *Strauder v. West Virginia* (1880). That decision laid the foundation for the Court's unceasing efforts to eradicate racial discrimination in the procedures used to select the venire [group of potential jurors] from which individual jurors are drawn. In *Strauder*, the Court explained that the central concern of the recently ratified Fourteenth Amendment was to put an end to governmental discrimination on account of race. Exclusion of black citizens from service as jurors constitutes a primary example of the evil the Fourteenth Amendment was designed to cure.

In holding that racial discrimination in jury selection offends the Equal Protection Clause, the Court in *Strauder* recognized, however, that a defendant has no right to a "petit jury composed in whole or in part of persons of his own race." "The number of our races and nationalities stands in the way of evolution of such a conception" of the demand of equal protection. *Akins v. Texas* (1945). But the defendant does have the right to be tried by a jury whose members are selected pursuant to nondiscriminatory criteria. *Martin v. Texas* (1906); *Ex parte Virginia* (1880). The Equal Protection Clause guarantees the defendant that the State will not exclude members of his race from the jury venire on account of race, *Strauder*, or on the false assumption that members of his race as a group are not qualified to serve as jurors, see *Norris v. Alabama* (1935); *Neal v. Delaware* (1881).

Racial Discrimination in Juries Undermines Confidence

Purposeful racial discrimination in selection of the venire violates a defendant's right to equal protection because it denies him the protection that a trial by jury is intended to secure. "The very idea of a jury is a body . . . composed of the

peers or equals of the person whose rights it is selected or
summoned to determine; that is, of his neighbors, fellows,
associates, persons having the same legal status in society as
that which he holds." *Strauder;* see *Carter v. Jury Comm'n of
Greene County* (1970). The petit jury has occupied a central
position in our system of justice by safeguarding a person accused of crime against the arbitrary exercise of power by
prosecutor or judge. *Duncan v. Louisiana* (1968). Those on
the venire must be "indifferently chosen," to secure the defendant's right under the Fourteenth Amendment to "protection of life and liberty against race or color prejudice."
Strauder.

Racial discrimination in selection of jurors harms not only
the accused whose life or liberty they are summoned to try.
Competence to serve as a juror ultimately depends on an assessment of individual qualifications and ability impartially
to consider evidence presented at a trial. See *Thiel v. Southern Pacific Co.* (1946). A person's race simply "is unrelated to
his fitness as a juror." (Frankfurter, J., dissenting). As long
ago as *Strauder*, therefore, the Court recognized that by denying a person participation in jury service on account of his
race, the State unconstitutionally discriminated against the
excluded juror; see *Carter v. Jury Comm'n of Greene County;
Neal v. Delaware.*

The harm from discriminatory jury selection extends beyond that inflicted on the defendant and the excluded juror
to touch the entire community. Selection procedures that purposefully exclude black persons from juries undermine public confidence in the fairness of our system of justice. See
Ballard v. United States (1946); *McCray v. New York* (1983)
(MARSHALL, J., dissenting from denial of certiorari). Discrimination within the judicial system is most pernicious because it is "a stimulant to that race prejudice which is an
impediment to securing to [black citizens] that equal justice
which the law aims to secure to all others." *Strauder.*

States Bound by Equal Protection Clause

In *Strauder*, the Court invalidated a state statute that provided that only white men could serve as jurors. We can be

confident that no State now has such a law. The Constitution requires, however, that we look beyond the face of the statute defining juror qualifications and also consider challenged selection practices to afford "protection against action of the State through its administrative officers in effecting the prohibited discrimination." *Norris v. Alabama;* see *Hernandez v. Texas* (1954); *Ex parte Virginia.* Thus, the Court has found a denial of equal protection where the procedures implementing a neutral statute operated to exclude persons from the venire on racial grounds, and has made clear that the Constitution prohibits all forms of purposeful racial discrimination in selection of jurors. While decisions of this Court have been concerned largely with discrimination during selection of the venire, the principles announced there also forbid discrimination on account of race in selection of the petit jury. Since the Fourteenth Amendment protects an accused throughout the proceedings bringing him to justice, *Hill v. Texas* (1942), the State may not draw up its jury lists pursuant to neutral procedures but then resort to discrimination at "other stages in the selection process," *Avery v. Georgia* (1953); see *McCray v. New York* (MARSHALL, J., dissenting from denial of certiorari); see also *Alexander v. Louisiana* (1972).

Accordingly, the component of the jury selection process at issue here, the State's privilege to strike individual jurors through peremptory challenges [dismissing jurors for unstated reasons], is subject to the commands of the Equal Protection Clause. Although a prosecutor ordinarily is entitled to exercise permitted peremptory challenges "for any reason at all, as long as that reason is related to his view concerning the outcome" of the case to be tried, *United States v. Robinson* (1976), *United States v. Newman* (1977), the Equal Protection Clause forbids the prosecutor to challenge potential jurors solely on account of their race or on the assumption that black jurors as a group will be unable impartially to consider the State's case against a black defendant.

The principles announced in *Strauder* never have been questioned in any subsequent decision of this Court. Rather, the Court has been called upon repeatedly to review the application of those principles to particular facts. A recurring question in these cases, as in any case alleging a violation of the Equal Protection Clause, was whether the defendant had met his burden of proving purposeful discrimination on the part of the State. *Whitus v. Georgia* (1967); *Hernandez v. Texas; Akins v. Texas; Martin v. Texas.* That question also was at the heart of the portion of *Swain v. Alabama* we reexamine today.

Equal Protection Clause Limits Peremptory Challenges

Swain required the Court to decide, among other issues, whether a black defendant was denied equal protection by the State's exercise of peremptory challenges to exclude members of his race from the petit jury. The record in *Swain* showed that the prosecutor had used the State's peremptory challenges to strike the six black persons included on the petit jury venire. While rejecting the defendant's claim for failure to prove purposeful discrimination, the Court nonetheless indicated that the Equal Protection Clause placed some limits on the State's exercise of peremptory challenges.

The Court sought to accommodate the prosecutor's historical privilege of peremptory challenge free of judicial control, and the constitutional prohibition on exclusion of persons from jury service on account of race. While the Constitution does not confer a right to peremptory challenges, those challenges traditionally have been viewed as one means of assuring the selection of a qualified and unbiased jury. To preserve the peremptory nature of the prosecutor's challenge, the Court in *Swain* declined to scrutinize his actions in a particular case by relying on a presumption that he properly exercised the State's challenges.

The Court went on to observe, however, that a State may not exercise its challenges in contravention of the Equal Protection Clause. It was impermissible for a prosecutor to use his challenges to exclude blacks from the jury "for reasons wholly unrelated to the outcome of the particular case on trial" or to deny to blacks "the same right and opportunity to participate in the administration of justice enjoyed by the white population." Accordingly, a black defendant could make out a prima facie [at first sight] case of purposeful discrimination on proof that the peremptory challenge system was "being perverted" in that manner. For example, an inference of purposeful discrimination would be raised on evidence that a prosecutor, "in case after case, whatever the circumstances, whatever the crime and whoever the defendant or the victim may be, is responsible for the removal of Negroes who have been selected as qualified jurors by the jury commissioners and who have survived challenges for cause, with the result that no Negroes ever serve on petit juries." Evidence offered by the defendant in *Swain* did not meet that standard. While the defendant showed that prosecutors in the jurisdiction had exercised their strikes to exclude blacks from the jury, he offered no proof of the circumstances under which prosecutors were responsible for striking black jurors beyond the facts of his own case.

Proving a Pattern of Discrimination Not Necessary

A number of lower courts following the teaching of *Swain* reasoned that proof of repeated striking of blacks over a number of cases was necessary to establish a violation of the Equal Protection Clause. Since this interpretation of *Swain* has placed on defendants a crippling burden of proof, prosecutors' peremptory challenges are now largely immune from constitutional scrutiny. We reject this evidentiary formulation as inconsistent with standards that have been developed since *Swain* for assessing a prima facie case under the Equal Protection Clause. . . .

Since the decision in *Swain*, this Court has recognized that a defendant may make a prima facie showing of purposeful racial discrimination in selection of the venire by relying solely on the facts concerning its selection in his case. These decisions are in accordance with the proposition, articulated in *Arlington Heights v. Metropolitan Housing Development Corp.*, that "a consistent pattern of official racial discrimination" is not "a necessary predicate to a violation of the Equal Protection Clause. A single invidiously discriminatory governmental act" is not "immunized by the absence of such discrimination in the making of other comparable decisions." For evidentiary requirements to dictate that "several must suffer discrimination" before one could object, *McCray v. New York*, would be inconsistent with the promise of equal protection to all. . . .

In deciding whether the defendant has made the requisite showing, the trial court should consider all relevant circumstances. For example, a "pattern" of strikes against black jurors included in the particular venire might give rise to an inference of discrimination. Similarly, the prosecutor's questions and statements during voir dire [jury selection] examination and in exercising his challenges may support or refute an inference of discriminatory purpose. These examples are merely illustrative. We have confidence that trial judges, experienced in supervising voir dire, will be able to decide if the circumstances concerning the prosecutor's use of peremptory challenges creates a prima facie case of discrimination against black jurors.

Once the defendant makes a prima facie showing, the burden shifts to the State to come forward with a neutral explanation for challenging black jurors. Though this requirement imposes a limitation in some cases on the full peremptory character of the historic challenge, we emphasize that the prosecutor's explanation need not rise to the level justifying exercise of a challenge for cause. See *McCray v. Abrams*; *Booker v. Jabe* (1985). But the prosecutor may not rebut the defendant's prima facie case of discrimination by stating merely that he challenged jurors of the defendant's race on the assumption—or his intuitive judgment—that they would be partial to the defendant because of their shared race. Cf. *Norris v. Alabama*, see *Thompson v. United States* (1984) (BRENNAN, J., dissenting from denial of certiorari). Just as the Equal Protection Clause forbids the States to exclude black persons from the venire on the assumption that blacks as a group are unqualified to serve as jurors, so it forbids the States to strike black veniremen on the assumption that they will be biased in a particular case simply because the defendant is black. The core guarantee of equal protection, ensuring citizens that their State will not discriminate on account of race, would be meaningless were we to approve the exclusion of jurors on the basis of such assumptions, which arise solely from the jurors' race. Nor may the prosecutor rebut the defendant's case merely by denying that he had a discriminatory motive or "affirm[ing] [his] good faith in making individual selections." *Alexander v. Louisiana.* If these general assertions were accepted as rebutting a defendant's prima facie case, the Equal Protection Clause "would be but a vain and illusory requirement." *Norris v. Alabama.* The prosecutor therefore must articulate a neutral explanation related to the particular case to be tried. The trial court then will have the duty to determine if the defendant has established purposeful discrimination. . . .

In this case [*Batson v. Kentucky*], petitioner made a timely objection to the prosecutor's removal of all black persons on the venire. Because the trial court flatly rejected the objection without requiring the prosecutor to give an explanation for his action, we remand this case for further proceedings. If the trial court decides that the facts establish, prima facie, purposeful discrimination and the prosecutor does not come forward with a neutral explanation for his action, our precedents require that petitioner's conviction be reversed.

CHAPTER THREE

Controversies and Perspectives on Trial by Jury

The Jury System Promotes Democracy

Alexis de Tocqueville

In 1831 a French aristocrat named Alexis de Tocqueville toured the young United States, ostensibly to study the U.S. prison system, but mainly to see "what a great republic is," as he told a friend in a letter. His nine months were well spent, with trips throughout all the states and the frontier provinces and meetings with such figures as Andrew Jackson, Daniel Webster, Sam Houston, and Charles Carroll, the last surviving signatory of the Declaration of Independence. The result was *Democracy in America*, published in two volumes in 1835 and 1840, a classic still cited by virtually every historian of American government, as well as presidents and political philosophers and anyone seeking a deeper understanding of the actual practice of democracy. While the work goes far beyond the original idea of studying prison reforms, de Tocqueville's insights into the American judicial system remain a vital part of his overall theme. In the excerpt below, he discusses the political impact of juries, which he sees as little schools of democracy. By familiarizing average people with the law and their rights, juries instill habits of mind that make Americans better voters and more self-confident citizens.

Since my subject has led me to speak of the administration of justice in the United States, I will not pass over it without adverting to the institution of the jury. Trial by jury may be considered in two separate points of view; as a judicial, and as a political institution. If it was my purpose to inquire how far trial by jury, especially in civil cases, insures a

Alexis de Tocqueville, *Democracy in America, Volume 1,* translated by Henry Reeve and edited by Francis Bowen. Cambridge, MA: Sever and Francis, 1863.

good administration of justice, I admit that its utility might be contested. As the jury was first established when society was in its infancy, and when courts of justice merely decided simple questions of fact, it is not an easy task to adapt it to the wants of a highly civilized community, when the mutual relations of men are multiplied to a surprising extent, and have assumed an enlightened and intellectual character.

My present purpose is to consider the jury as a political institution; any other course would divert me from my subject. Of trial by jury, considered as a judicial institution, I shall here say but little. When the English adopted trial by jury, they were a semi-barbarous people; they have since become one of the most enlightened nations of the earth; and their attachment to this institution seems to have increased with their increasing cultivation. They have emigrated and colonized every part of the habitable globe; some have formed colonies, others independent states; the mother country has maintained its monarchical constitution; many of its offspring have founded powerful republics; but everywhere they have boasted of the privilege of trial by jury. They have established it, or hastened to re-establish it, in all their settlements. A judicial institution which thus obtains the suffrages of a great people for so long a series of ages, which is zealously reproduced at every stage of civilization, in all the climates of the earth, and under every form of human government, cannot be contrary to the spirit of justice.

Juries as a Political Institution

But to leave this part of the subject. It would be a very narrow view to look upon the jury as a mere judicial institution; for, however great its influence may be upon the decisions of the courts, it is still greater on the destinies of society at large. The jury is, above all, a political institution, and it must be regarded in this light in order to be duly appreciated.

By the jury, I mean a certain number of citizens chosen by lot, and invested with a temporary right of judging. Trial by jury, as applied to the repression of crime, appears to me an eminently republican element in the government, for the following reasons.

The institution of the jury may be aristocratic or democratic, according to the class from which the jurors are taken; but it always preserves its republican character, in that it places the real direction of society in the hands of the governed, or of a portion of the governed, and not in that of the government. Force is never more than a transient element of success, and after force, comes the notion of right. A government which should be able to reach its enemies only upon a field of battle would soon be destroyed. The true sanction of political laws is to be found in penal legislation; and if that sanction be wanting, the law will sooner or later lose its cogency. He who punishes the criminal is therefore the real master of society. Now, the institution of the jury raises the people itself, or at least a class of citizens, to the bench of judges. The institution of the jury consequently invests the people, or that class of citizens, with the direction of society.

Alexis de Tocqueville

Different Governments Have Different Juries

In England, the jury is returned from the aristocratic portion of the nation; the aristocracy makes the laws, applies the laws, and punishes infractions of the laws everything is established upon a consistent footing, and England may with truth be said to constitute an aristocratic republic. In the United States, the same system is applied to the whole people. Every American citizen is qualified to be an elector, a juror, and is eligible to office. The system of the jury, as it is understood in America, appears to me to be as direct and as extreme a consequence of the sovereignty of the people as universal suffrage. They are two instruments of equal power, which contribute to the supremacy of the majority. All the sovereigns who have chosen to govern by their own authority, and to direct society instead of obeying its directions, have destroyed or enfeebled the institution of the jury. The Tudor monarchs sent to prison jurors who refused to convict, and Napoleon caused them to be selected by his agents.

However clear most of these truths may seem to be, they do not command universal assent; and, in France at least, the trial by jury is still but imperfectly understood. If the question arises as to the proper qualification of jurors, it is confined to a discussion of the intelligence and knowledge of the citizens who may be returned, as if the jury was merely a judicial institution. This appears to me the least important part of the subject. The jury is pre-eminently a political institution; it should be regarded as one form of the sovereignty of the people: when that sovereignty is repudiated, it must be rejected, or it must be adapted to the laws by which that sovereignty is established. The jury is that portion of the nation to which the execution of the laws is intrusted, as the legislature is that part of the nation which makes the laws; and in order that society may be governed in a fixed and uniform manner the list of citizens qualified to serve on juries must increase and diminish with the list of electors. This I hold to be the point of view most worthy of the attention of the legislator; all that remains is merely accessory.

Civil Juries Equally Important

I am so entirely convinced that the jury is pre-eminently a political institution, that I still consider it in this light when it is applied in civil causes. Laws are always unstable unless they are founded upon the manners of a nation: manners are the only durable and resisting power in a people. When the jury is reserved for criminal offences, the people only witness its occasional action in particular cases: they become accustomed to do without it in the ordinary course of life; and it is considered as an instrument, but not as the only instrument, of obtaining justice. This is true *a fortiori*, when the jury is applied only to certain criminal causes.

When, on the contrary, the jury acts also on civil causes, its application is constantly visible; it affects all the interests of the community; every one co-operates in its work: it thus penetrates into all the usages of life, it fashions the human mind to its peculiar forms, and is gradually associated with the idea of justice itself.

The institution of the jury, if confined to criminal causes, is always in danger; but when once it is introduced into civil proceedings, it defies the aggressions of time and man. If it had been as easy to remove the jury from the manners as from the laws of England, it would have perished under the Tudors; and the civil jury did in reality, at that period, save the liberties of England. In whatever manner the jury be applied, it cannot fail to exercise a powerful influence upon the national character; but this influence is prodigiously increased when it is introduced into civil causes. The jury, and more especially the civil jury, serves to communicate the spirit of the judges to the minds of all the citizens; and this spirit, with the habits which attend it, is the soundest preparation for free institutions. It imbues all classes with a respect for the thing judged, and with the notion of right. If these two elements be removed, the love of independence becomes a mere destructive passion. It teaches men to practise equity; every man learns to judge his neighbor as he would himself be judged. And this is especially true of the jury in civil causes; for, whilst the number of persons who have reason to apprehend a criminal prosecution is small, every one is liable to have a lawsuit. The jury teaches every man not to recoil before the responsibility of his own actions, and impresses him with that manly confidence without which no political virtue can exist. It invests each citizen with a kind of magistracy; it makes them all feel the duties which they are bound to discharge towards society, and the part which they take in its government. By obliging men to turn their attention to other affairs than their own, it rubs off that private selfishness which is the rust of society.

Juries as a Public School

The jury contributes powerfully to form the judgment and to increase the natural intelligence of a people; and this, in my opinion, is its greatest advantage. It may be regarded as a gratuitous public school, ever open, in which every juror learns his rights, enters into daily communication with the most learned and enlightened members of the upper classes, and becomes practically acquainted with the laws, which are brought within the reach of his capacity by the efforts of the bar, the advice of the judge, and even by the passions of the parties. I think that the practical intelligence and political good sense of the Americans are mainly attributable to the long use which they have made of the jury in civil causes.

I do not know whether the jury is useful to those who have lawsuits; but I am certain it is highly beneficial to those who judge them; and I look upon it as one of the most efficacious means for the education of the people which society can employ.

Juries Enhance the Power of Judges

What I have said applies to all nations; but the remark I am about to make is peculiar to the Americans and to democratic communities. I have already observed that, in democracies, the members of the legal profession, and the judicial magistrates, constitute the only aristocratic body which can moderate the movement of the people. This aristocracy is invested with no physical power; it exercises its conservative influence upon the minds of men: and the most abundant source of its authority is the institution of the civil jury. In criminal causes, when society is contending against a single man, the jury is apt to look upon the judge as the passive instrument of social power, and to mistrust his advice. Moreover, criminal causes turn entirely upon simple facts, which common sense can readily appreciate; upon this ground, the judge and the jury are equal. Such, however, is not the case in civil causes; then the judge appears as a disinterested arbiter between the conflicting passions of the parties. The jurors look up to him with confidence, and listen to him with respect, for in this instance, his intellect entirely governs theirs. It is the judge who sums up the various arguments which have wearied their memory, and who guides them through the devious course of the proceedings; he points their attention to the exact question of fact, which they are called upon to decide, and tells them how to answer the question of law. His influence over them is almost unlimited.

If I am called upon to explain why I am but little moved by the arguments derived from the ignorance of jurors in civil causes, I reply, that in these proceedings, whenever the question to be solved is not a mere question of fact, the jury has only the semblance of a judicial body. The jury only sanctions the decision of the judge; they sanction this decision by the authority of society which they represent, and he, by that of reason and of law.

Influence of Judges Beyond Courtroom

In England and in America, the judges exercise an influence upon criminal trials which the French judges have never possessed. The reason of this difference may easily be discovered; the English and American magistrates have established their authority in civil causes, and only transfer it afterwards to tribunals of another kind, where it was not first acquired. In some cases, and they are frequently the most important ones, the American judges have the right of deciding causes alone. Upon these occasions, they are accidentally placed in the position which the French judges habitually occupy: but their moral power is much greater; they are still surrounded by the recollection of the jury, and their judgment has almost as much authority as the voice of the community represented by that institution. Their influence extends far beyond the limits of the courts; in the recreations of private life, as well as in the turmoil of public business, in public and in the legislative assemblies, the American judge is constantly surrounded by men who are accustomed to regard his intelligence as superior to their own; and after having exercised his power in the decision of causes, he continues to influence the habits of thought, and even the characters, of those who acted with him in his official capacity. The jury, then, which seems to restrict the rights of the judiciary, does in reality consolidate its power; and in no country are the judges so powerful as where the people share their privileges. It is especially by means of the jury in civil causes, that the American magistrates imbue even the lower classes of society with the spirit of their profession. Thus the jury, which is the most energetic means of making the people rule, is also the most efficacious means of teaching it how to rule well.

Juries Must Judge the Validity of the Laws

Lysander Spooner

In his impassioned treatise *An Essay on the Trial by Jury*, Lysander Spooner set forth the notion that juries must have the ability to judge the law as well as the facts, a controversial theory known today as "jury nullification." Spooner himself was a veteran of numerous courtroom battles with government and the judicial establishment. In the 1830s he set up shop as a lawyer after three years of study, in open defiance of the Massachusetts legislature's provision that non–college graduates should have five years of study with an attorney before going independent. In 1844 he started his own private mail service, challenging the monopoly power of the U.S. Post Office. In addition, he was a staunch abolitionist who urged jurors not to convict anyone under the Fugitive Slave Act, which stipulated that runaway slaves should be returned to their Southern masters. In court and in a series of pamphlets, Spooner had established himself as a vigorous opponent of governmental oppression in all its varieties, even seeing the Constitution itself as a threat to mankind's natural liberties. In the following excerpt, Spooner sets forth his belief that juries must assess not only guilt or innocence, but also the admissibility of evidence, the propriety of the jury selection process, and the justice of the law itself. His position is a radical departure from the prevailing view of the role of juries in contemporary trials. Nevertheless, it is a perspective shared by many individuals and organizations who support the concept of "jury nullification"—the idea that juries can refuse to uphold laws they deem unjust.

Lysander Spooner, *An Essay on the Trial by Jury*. Boston: John P. Jewett, 1852.

For more than six hundred years—that is, since Magna Carta, in 1215—there has been no clearer principle of English or American constitutional law, than that, in criminal cases, it is not only the right and duty of juries to judge what are the facts, what is the law, and what was the moral intent of the accused; *but that it is also their right, and their primary and paramount duty, to judge of the justice of the law, and to hold all laws invalid, that are, in their opinion, unjust or oppressive, and all persons guiltless in violating, or resisting the execution of, such laws.*

Unless such be the right and duty of jurors, it is plain that, instead of juries being a "palladium of liberty"—a barrier against the tyranny and oppression of the government—they are really mere tools in its hands, for carrying into execution any injustice and oppression it may desire to have executed.

But for their right to judge of the law, *and the justice of the law*, juries would be no protection to an accused person, *even as to matters of fact;* for, if the government can dictate to a jury any law whatever, in a criminal case, it can certainly dictate to them the laws of evidence. That is, it can dictate what evidence is admissible, and what inadmissible, *and also what force or weight is to be given to the evidence admitted.* And if the government can thus dictate to a jury the laws of evidence, it can not only make it necessary for them to convict on a partial exhibition of the evidence rightfully pertaining to the case, but it can even require them to convict on any evidence whatever that it pleases to offer them.

Real Objective of Trial by Jury

That the rights and duties of jurors must necessarily be such as are here claimed for them, will be evident when it is considered what the trial by jury is, and what is its object.

"The trial by jury," then, *is a "trial by the country"—that is, by the people—as distinguished from a trial by the government.*

It was anciently called "trial *per pais"*—that is, "trial by the country." And now, in every criminal trial, the jury are told that the accused "has, for trial, put himself upon the *country*; which *country* you (the jury) are."

The object of this trial "by the country," or by the people, in preference to a trial by the government, is to guard against every species of oppression by the government. In order to effect this end, it is indispensable that the people, or "the country," judge of and determine their own liberties against the government; instead of the government's judging of and determining its own powers over the people. How is it possible that juries can do anything to protect the liberties of the people against the government, if they are not allowed to determine what those liberties are?

How Freedom Is Preserved

Any government, that is its own judge of, and determines authoritatively for the people, what are its own powers over the people, is an absolute government of course. It has all the powers that it chooses to exercise. There is no other—or at least no more accurate—definition of a despotism than this.

On the other hand, any people, that judge of, and determine authoritatively for the government, what are their own liberties against the government, of course retain all the liberties they wish to enjoy. *And this is freedom.* At least, it is freedom *to them*; because, although it may be theoretically imperfect, it, nevertheless, corresponds to *their* highest notions of freedom.

To secure this right of the people to judge of their own liberties against the government, the jurors are taken, (or must be, to make them lawful jurors,) from the body of the people, *by lot*, or by some process that precludes any previous knowledge, choice, or selection of them, on the part of the government. This is done to prevent the government's constituting a jury of its own partisans or friends; in other words, to prevent the government's *packing* a jury, with a view to maintain its own laws, and accomplish its own purposes.

Representative Jurors

It is supposed that, if twelve men be taken, *by lot*, from the mass of the people, without the possibility of any previous knowledge, choice, or selection of them, on the part of the government, the jury will be a fair epitome of "the country" at large, and not merely of the party or faction that sustain the measures of the government; that substantially all classes of opinions, prevailing among the people, will be represented in the jury; and especially that the opponents of the government, (if the government have any opponents,) will be represented there, as well as its friends; that the classes, who are oppressed by the laws of the government, (if any are thus oppressed,) will have their representatives in the jury, as well as those classes, who take sides with the oppressor—that is, with the government.

It is fairly presumable that such a tribunal will agree to no conviction except such as *substantially the whole country* would agree to, if they were present, taking part in the trial. A trial by such a tribunal is, therefore, in effect, "a trial by the country." In its results it probably comes as near to a trial by the whole country, as any trial that it is practicable to have, without too great inconvenience and expense. And as unanimity is required for a conviction, it follows that no one can be convicted, except for the violation of such laws as substantially the *whole* country wish to have maintained. The government can enforce none of its laws, (by punishing offenders, through the verdicts of juries,) except such as substantially the whole people wish to have enforced. The government, therefore, consistently with the trial by jury, can exercise no powers over the people, (or, what is the same thing, over the accused person, who represents the rights of the people,) except such as substantially the whole people of the country consent that it may exercise. In such a trial, therefore, "the country," or the people, judge of and determine their own liberties against the government, instead of the government's judging of and determining its own powers over the people.

But all this "trial by the country" would be no trial at all "by the country," but only a trial by the government, if the government could either declare who may, and who may not, be jurors, or could dictate to the jury anything whatever, either of law or evidence, that is of the essence of the trial.

Government Should Not Pick Jurors

If the government may decide who may, and who may not, be jurors, it will of course select only its partisans, and those friendly to its measures. It may not only prescribe who may, and who may not, be eligible to be drawn as jurors; but it may also question each person drawn as a juror, as to his sentiments in regard to the particular law involved in each trial, before suffering him to be sworn on the panel; and exclude him if he be found unfavorable to the maintenance of such a law.

So, also, if the government may dictate to the jury *what laws they are to enforce*, it is no longer a "trial by the country," but a trial by the government; because the jury then try the accused, not by any standard of their own—not by their own judgments of their rightful liberties—but by a standard dictated to them by the government. And the standard, thus dictated by the government, becomes the measure of the people's liberties. If the government dictate the standard of trial, it of course dictates the results of the trial. And such a trial is no trial by the country, but only a trial by the government; and in it the government determines what are its own powers over the people, instead of the people's determining what are their own liberties against the government. In short, if the jury have no right to judge of the justice of a law of the government, they plainly can do nothing to protect the people against the oppressions of the government; for there are no oppressions which the government may not authorize by law.

Necessary Powers of Juries

The jury are also to judge whether the laws are rightly expounded to them by the court. Unless they judge on this point, they do nothing to protect their liberties against the oppressions that are capable of being practised under cover of a corrupt exposition of the laws. If the judiciary can authoritatively dictate to a jury any exposition of the law, they can dictate to them the law itself, and such laws as they please; because laws are, in practice, one thing or another, according as they are expounded.

The jury must also judge whether there really be any such law, (be it good or bad,) as the accused is charged with having transgressed. Unless they judge on this point, the people are liable to have their liberties taken from them by brute force, without any law at all.

The jury must also judge of the laws of evidence. If the government can dictate to a jury the laws of evidence, it can not only shut out any evidence it pleases, tending to vindicate the accused, but it can require that any evidence whatever, that it pleases to offer, be held as conclusive proof of any offence whatever which the government chooses to allege.

Jury Must Judge the Whole Case

It is manifest, therefore, that the jury must judge of and try the whole case, and every part and parcel of the case, free of any dictation or authority on the part of the government. They must judge of the existence of the law; of the true exposition of the law; *of the justice of the law*; and of the admissibility and weight of all the evidence offered; otherwise the government will have everything its own way; the jury will be mere puppets in the hands of the government; and the trial will be, in reality, a trial by the government, and not a "trial by the country." By such trials the government will determine its own powers over the people, instead of the people's determining their own liberties against the government; and it will be an entire delusion to talk, as for centuries we have done, of the trial by jury, as a "palladium of liberty," or as any protection to the people against the oppression and tyranny of the government.

The question, then, between trial by jury, as thus described, and trial by the government, is simply a question between liberty and despotism. The authority to judge what are the powers of the government, and what the liberties of the people, must necessarily be vested in one or the other of the parties themselves—the government, or the people; because there is no third party to whom it can be entrusted. If the authority be vested in the government, the government is absolute, and the people have no liberties except such as the government sees fit to indulge them with. If, on the other hand, that authority be vested in the people, then the people have all liberties, (as against the government,) except such as substantially the whole people (through a jury) choose to disclaim; and the government can exercise no power except such as substantially the whole people (through a jury) consent that it may exercise.

Juries Should Not Be Abolished in Civil Cases

Paula DiPerna

When writer Paula DiPerna was called for jury service but not selected to serve, she decided to sit through the trial anyway. Throughout the proceedings she interviewed the lawyers, and afterward she talked to the jurors. The result was a fascination with the jury system and its profound strengths and weaknesses, which grew into her book *Juries on Trial: Faces of American Justice.* In the excerpt below she discusses the various dynamics that affect civil juries, the ways lawyers use and sometimes misuse these juries, and the misconceptions that some commentators have about the civil jury system, especially when a jury awards a plaintiff a seemingly outrageous amount. For DiPerna, while alternatives such as arbitration have their place, the right to present one's case to an impartial jury remains a vital defense for victims of injustice.

O ften, the jury has to decide the monetary value of a person's life. In the case of Robert Williams, aged twenty-five, who was killed by a robotic vehicle in a Ford Motor Company casting plant in Flat Rock, Michigan, on January 25, 1979, the jury awarded his family $10 million. Almost immediately after the verdict was announced, in August 1983, the attorney for the defendant company, which designed the robot, filed a motion for a judgment notwithstanding the verdict—a reduction of the verdict award, or a new trial—calling the jury's verdict a "shock to the judicial conscience."

Paula DiPerna, *Juries on Trial: Faces of American Justice.* New York: Dembner, 1984. Copyright © 1984 by Paula DiPerna. Reproduced by permission of the publisher.

It was a typical complaint in an atypical case, and typically the jury bore the brunt of the criticism. However, judicial conscience and community conscience may not have been parallel in this case. That is why there is a jury system in civil law, and why some critics contend the civil jury is a remnant of the past.

It took only a few hours to select the jury in the case of Sandra A. Williams, administratrix of the estate of Robert N. Williams, versus Unit Handling Systems, a division of Litton Industries, Inc., the system's designer. There were no challenges for cause, very little questioning about the jurors' backgrounds or personal beliefs. Though the case was heard in state court, all questions during voir dire were posed by the judge. The attorneys, though they could have put additional questions to the jurors through the judge, opted to seat the six-person jury with a minimum of delay, although the nature of the case might well have drowned voir dire in detail.

Robert Williams died instantly when he was struck in the head by the mechanical arm of a robot, designed by Litton and installed at the Ford plant, which produced sand cores for molding the hollow places in engine blocks. The legal questions were simple: Who, if anyone, was negligent and who, if anyone, was liable? But in determining that, the jury which heard the case also was grappling with questions of how machines—computers and robots—will interact, legally speaking, with workers in the future. It was a case that brought into sharp relief how community attitudes and economic circumstances seep into the justice system and how the jury functions in civil law.

Had the case been heard by a judge alone, the verdict might not have been as astronomical. However, the jury's presence converted the episode into an event with wide ramifications for industrial policy, which policy makers might study. Whether six people on a jury should have such influence is part of the recurrent argument over whether juries should be abolished in civil cases. The Williams case demonstrates what might be lost and what might be gained by abolition.

Millions of civil cases are litigated each year in the United States—everything from broken sidewalk cases to billion-dollar antitrust suits. Much is written and said about the "litigation explosion" and excessive jury awards. In his 1949 book *Courts on Trial*, Jerome Frank wrote that in civil matters "trial by jury seriously interferes with correct—and therefore just—decisions." Chief Justice Warren Burger has advocated abolishing the jury in civil matters. Hans Zeisel believes it is possible that the civil jury could be gone before the end of the century because it is "much less firmly rooted in Constitutional guarantees."

However, as one lawyer expressed it, the jury is an "easy target," because it decides the outcome; and those who do not like the outcome often blame the jury for having done some wrong. Interestingly only a fraction of the cases filed ever come to trial—approximately 6 percent in the federal system. . . .

High Awards Lead to Questioning Jury System

Clearly, something has changed in terms of what juries consider fair settlements. In 1962, nationwide, only one jury verdict awarded $1 million or more in personal injury suits. In 1981, there were 235 such awards.

Critics of jury settlements often evaluate those settlements in the vacuum of the trial court, where the jurors are supposed to be immune to aspects of the outside world that might influence them. However, in Detroit, the social and economic context from which the jury derives is extremely difficult to set aside. Detroit, long a symbol of the industrial prowess of the United States, embodied in the automobile industry, is now a symbol of the decline of that prowess. Downtown Detroit may have a Renaissance Center, but it also has the huge space left empty by Hudson's Department Store, the last great retail establishment to abandon the inner city. As jurors drive to and from court each day, they often must traverse whole blocks of ghetto, constantly aware of how much the city has depended on industry and how much industry has proved undependable. Though there are signs of recovery in some areas, the efforts seem so earnest as to be desperate. A billboard outside a row of new downtown apartments, for example, proclaims in silver letters that glisten in the sun, "Buy a condominium. Get a Cadillac free."

Critics of the Williams verdict think his family got the equivalent of a free Cadillac. Tonkin, the Litton attorney, while in no way belittling the tragedy of the death, says he expected a verdict no higher than $2.5 million. He filed a judgment notwithstanding the verdict, under laws which permit this as a redress of jury error if a verdict is thought to have been reckless or not based on fact.

Juries Accused of Not Understanding

Often in civil cases, when the jury verdict is in dispute, there are accusations that the jury really did not understand the case or the nuances of the law, and that error and sympathy conspire in favor of the plaintiff. Though Litton's attorney argued in his motion that the verdict rendered by the jury was against the great weight of the evidence and was based upon "conjecture, speculation and guess . . . with no basis in fact," he would not wish to see the jury eliminated. "The jury system is fair, although perhaps I shouldn't say this, but I would do better as a defendant's lawyer without it. It is a heavy burden upon a judge to decide a case like this. I am not so sure that in a routine case a judge would be better than a jury. This case was an exception. You don't see these verdicts every day."

As to whether the verdict was incorrect—that is, not based on evidence—one must look to the nature of the adversary system. The Williams jury foreman noted, "The judge just sits up there and lets some of these lawyers carry on maybe a little too much. Watching witnesses is very enlightening. If it is their lawyer examining them, it is one thing; then when the other lawyer comes up, they automatically, just like day and night, they just flip their style." He also added, "You can see there's always some points the lawyers on both sides would just as soon not develop." It is what Jerome Frank called the "'fight' theory versus the 'truth' theory of the law," and it is the battle which takes place in every courtroom in the United States.

Though both attorneys agree that the Williams case was "clean"—that is, undertaken with a minimum of lawyerly tactical warfare—there are certainly two views of the truth in this case. Litton's view held that their system was safely designed if used as recommended, and the Williams' view was that Litton's idea of how the system would be used never meshed with the practical circumstances of its operation. Each side buttressed its view with legal references and other case law, but in the end, the jury's view of the facts lined up with the plaintiff—save for the lone dissenter, who matched up squarely with the defense. So, the jurors understood the arguments and did what they were charged to do—namely, determine where they felt the preponderance of the evidence fell. . . .

Of course, most civil cases are routine and well within the grasp of the average juror, and, most often, the jury performs at least as well as in criminal matters and similarly to the judge. The Kalven-Zeisel study in 1966 of over 4,000 civil cases found that judges and juries agreed about liability in 78 percent of the cases, and, perhaps more interesting, the jury was more favorable to the plaintiff in 12 percent of the remaining cases while the judge was more favorable in 10 percent of them. As Kalven and Zeisel wrote, "This finding is in the teeth of the popular expectation that the jury in personal injury cases favors the plaintiff, at least if that expectation is taken to mean that the jury is more likely to favor the plaintiff than is the judge." The study does add, however, that "when it comes to the issue of damages, the jury's award is on the average about 20 percent higher than that of the judge." In 1937, in the six-county study including Wayne, practically no difference was found in the assessment of damages between judge and jury, which may mean a slight shift has taken place, more indicative of society's attitudes toward money and who should have it, than to efficiency of the jury system. But if juries are likely to award more than is a judge, that seems to be part of the contemporary process of litigation, and the jury system per se should not be penalized because of differing views of what various damages are worth. It seems to me that if we are content to let the market decide what food, clothing, and housing should cost, we ought to be content to allow the market—the jury—decide what value to place on injuries, inconvenience, and wrongful death.

Juries as Pawns

Whether or not the jury is statistically more likely to award higher damages, lawyers seem to act as though that were so. I have come to call this the "hot body" approach to justice, a phrase I picked up from a sagacious jury clerk in Manhattan. I had complained about being held in the bullpen, one of the large waiting rooms, without being called anywhere near a courtroom for a case and without any information about when I might be needed. "Relax," the clerk told me, "you don't think you are being used, but you are—just by breathing. You wouldn't believe how many cases have been settled this morning without coming to trial. When these lawyers see all you hot bodies out here, they decide to give in." What he meant, of course, was that pressured by the sight of a real jury ready to go, the side with the weaker case decided not to risk the jury trial at all but to settle for what was offered.

Often, too, a trial will begin, and as the lawyers see the case unfold, how their witnesses are coming across, how their side of the truth is holding up, they decide whether or not to go all the way to a verdict. This "use" of juries annoys most jurors, if mail I have received is any indication; for example: " . . . needless to say, the case that I finally ended up on was settled after three days of trial, two hour lunches for all of us and lots of taxpayers' money." And from an attorney in New Jersey:

"About six years ago I was involved in a very complex jury trial . . . about nine lawyers involved representing the various clients. . . . The jury selection alone droned on for two full weeks—intentionally so on the part of the [defense] lawyers to wear down the plaintiff in the case. . . . In the end, the case was settled shortly after the two weeks it took to pick the jury. The strategy worked. There was talk of all of us having reunions and getting T-shirts imprinted as a remembrance of the occasion. I really don't need the T-shirt to remember." Doubtless, neither do the jurors.

Eleventh-Hour Settlements

According to *Time* magazine in 1982, one quarter to one half of all cases that come before a jury are settled before the trial ends.

One young woman recounted the typical eleventh-hour tale. She had been selected as a juror in New York City in a case involving an incident that took place during the 1980 transit strike, which left the city's 9 million people without any public bus or subway service. In such emergencies, the city acquires the atmosphere of carnival, where routine is broken and one catches as catch can. In this atmosphere, the plaintiff rode a chartered bus toward his home but got off early because traffic was so snarled. At the corner, he claimed, he was offered a ride in his direction by the driver of a van owned by a dry cleaning company. However, before the plaintiff could enter the van, the vehicle started to pull away, knocking him down. A third vehicle—another chartered bus carrying employees of a large credit card company—allegedly ran into the man as he fell. The man broke a leg and sued the owners of both the van and the bus, which he claimed ran him down.

The trial lasted a week, and on the day the jury was about to begin deliberating, they noticed that the van company representative and his attorney were no longer in court. The judge instructed the jury to draw no inference from that— the juror told me the jury did not. After deliberating three hours the jury exonerated the bus company completely: "We did not believe it was possible to be run over by a bus and have only a broken leg." And it found the van company liable for $100,000. But then the jury learned that the van company had settled the case the day before by paying $40,000.

Tales such as these draw a lot of criticism to the jury system, based on the belief that if cases were tried before a judge, lawyers would be less cavalier about settling midway through or less likely to embark on trial of a less than worthy case. Also, the time taken up by jury selection would, in theory, be saved. Delay is an anathema to judicial efficiency advocates; and it is repeatedly argued that removing juries in civil cases would significantly reduce delay.

Interested in investigating popular assumptions about the jury system, Hans Zeisel set out in 1959 to look into whether time could be saved by eliminating juries. The conclusion of the study, based on New York's courts, was that it takes about 40 percent less time, overall, to try a personal injury case without a jury than with one. However, translating this "savings" into actual court conditions could in fact liberate only the equivalent of 1.5 judges because so few cases actually come to jury trial. A judge's calendar is consumed by many judicial functions in addition to jury trials. . . .

Removing Juries Not the Answer

While removing the jury would obviously eliminate the possibility of juror error, it would be an abuse of the idea of efficiency to use jury elimination to "scare away" unworthy suits or million-dollar verdicts. That seems to me to force the worthy suer to pay, in loss of the opportunity to put his cases before a representative group on its merits.

It would be more fairly efficient to provide alternatives to courts—arbitration, mediation. A good professional lawyer does not take a case to court for the heck of it, but removing the jury system will not remove poor unprofessional lawyers or judges.

Nor will it remove greed, which is an undeniable motive in some cases. Clients can be greedy, lawyers can be greedy, refusing to make offers of settlement, refusing to accept them. These greeds can feed each other, since the lawyers' fees are tied to, and often paid from, the settlement awarded.

The irony of civil law today is exemplified by the Williams case. In Michigan, there is an innovative system of mediation wherein a case comes before a panel of three attorneys who rotate, in their own form of jury duty, and make a recommendation for disposition to the parties involved. In the Williams case, the mediation panel recommended that Litton's Unit Handling division settle the case for $700,000. The plaintiff was willing to accept it, but Litton Industries was unwilling to pay it, electing to go on to trial, apparently against the advice of its local counsel. Consequently the defendant faced a $10 million liability verdict delivered by a jury the defendant had a part in selecting and chose, on its own, to appear in judgment before. And society might well be grateful that contemporary civil law is still able, through the jury, to give voice to those values which, though they must be expressed in terms of dollar amounts, really do transcend them.

The Criminal Jury Should Be Abolished

Michael Lind

In 1994 former football star O.J. Simpson was arrested and charged with murdering his ex-wife Nicole Brown Simpson and her friend Ronald Goldman. After a lengthy, racially divisive trial, Simpson was acquitted of the crimes. Many commentators were outraged by the not guilty verdict. For some, the problem went right to the heart of the criminal justice system: the jury. The jurors were criticized as biased, ignorant, unreasonable, and hopelessly unprepared for the complexities of DNA evidence and other modern methods of criminal forensics. Michael Lind, a senior fellow at the New America Foundation and the author of numerous political studies, including *The Next American Nation* and *The Radical Center: The Future of American Politics*, goes beyond the particular criticisms of the Simpson jurors to condemn the institution itself. He asserts that trial by jury is a barbaric hangover from medieval England, which separated itself from the more sensible traditions of Roman law, the basis of the civil law tradition on the European continent. For Lind, a panel of judges and trained professionals, with full information and long experience, would be much more likely to reach a just verdict than a jury that is subjected to various legal tricks and often prevented from hearing vital pieces of evidence.

In the days and weeks to come [following O.J. Simpson's acquittal], you will read and hear a small army of eminent jurists, politicians and journalists responding with soothing assurances to popular outrage over the travesty of justice in

Michael Lind, "Jury Dismissed," *The New Republic,* October 23, 1995. Copyright © 1995 by The New Republic, Inc. Reproduced by permission.

the Simpson case. They will tell you that, though fallible individuals sometimes make mistakes, the contemporary
American jury system remains the best arrangement ever
devised for ascertaining guilt and innocence. The jury system works.

Don't believe a word of it. The American jury system does
not work to free the innocent and punish the guilty in an efficient and humane manner. It never has. Juries have always
abused the institution, sacrificing impartial justice to political
or ethnic goals. In Colonial America, the jury gave colonists a
way to subvert local overlords appointed by London. From independence until the civil rights revolution, the jury was a
means by which white bigots legally lynched Indians, blacks
and Asians (or acquitted their white murderers). Today urban
black juries all too often put race above justice in the same
manner.

Even in a society less racially polarized than ours, the
Anglo-American jury system would be a bad idea. The
progress of civilization can be measured by the distance between the idea of crime as a matter between the criminal and
his victim's relatives (the feud, *wergild*), and the idea of crime
as an offense against the impersonal, constitutional state.
The twelve-person jury, which the Vikings bequeathed to
Anglo-Saxon England, lies on the barbaric end of the spectrum. For all the refinements of the past millennium, the
jury system bears the marks of its primitive origins. There's
the magical number twelve (about which irrational debates
occasionally erupt when the idea of ten- or eleven-member
panels is suggested). And there's the competition between attorneys and the ritual of cross-examination, which resemble,
respectively, trial by combat and torture (both of which, come
to think of it, were also jurisprudential approaches of the ancient Teutons [Germans]).

The Civil-Law Alternative

Though the news may come as a surprise, juries as we know
them are limited to the English-speaking, common-law world.
Most other Western democracies have inherited their system
of criminal justice from the continental European civil-law

(Roman law) tradition. The contemporary civil-law tradition is not, as Anglo-American propaganda would have it, one of authoritarian, "inquisitorial" justice, with all-powerful judges railroading helpless innocents. On the contrary, all civil-law democracies today provide for some form of trial by jury. In civil-law countries, however, the jury is typically made up of a small number of professional and lay judges. The professional judges bring their experience to bear in sifting the evidence; the lay judges prevent the professionals from acting on the basis of prejudice or politics. Yet another professional judge presides over the trial (in some countries, impartiality is further assured by three-judge tribunals).

The differences between the common-law and the civil-law approaches to criminal justice do not end with the composition of the jury. Grotesque battles over the admissibility of evidence . . . just do not occur in the civil-law world, where the trial is usually preceded by a relatively calm investigation and examination under the direction of the public prosecutor and an examining judge. The defendant is treated more fairly, in these early phases, than in the United States. According to Stanford Law professor John Henry Merryman in his study *The Civil Law Tradition*, "The dossier compiled by the examining magistrate is open to inspection by the defense, routinely providing information about the prosecution's case that in an American proceeding would be unavailable to the defense until its production was compelled by a motion for discovery or it was revealed at the trial." No surprise witnesses, no sealed evidence envelopes, no sleazy tricks during discovery. Suppose that the United States, like France and Germany, had adopted its own national version of the civil-law system in the eighteenth or nineteenth century, in place of the British common-law inheritance—an American Civil Code, like the Code Napoleon or the Prussian Code.

Suppose, furthermore, that O.J. Simpson had been tried for murder under civil-law rules. How likely is it that the Simpson trial, in those circumstances, would have degenerated into an appalling spectacle of dirty tricks and bizarre legal hairsplitting? How likely is it that Johnnie Cochran [Simpson's lawyer] would have played the race card and asked the jury to send a message to the L.A. police, if the jury had consisted of, say, Judge [Lance] Ito and several other professional magistrates, as well as a few laymen? And the outcome of the Simpson case in a civil-law America? According to professor Merryman, "a statement made by an eminent comparative scholar after long and careful study is instructive: he said that if he were innocent, he would prefer to be tried by a civil-law court, but that if he were guilty, he would prefer to be tried by a common-law court."

Americans Should Set Aside Pride

I realize, of course, that by suggesting that we Americans might actually learn something from other countries I am questioning the dogma that the political and legal system of the United States has been perfect since its immaculate conception in an act of collective parthenogenesis by the Founding Fathers. The rules of American public discourse hold that no innovation in government or jurisprudence unknown to Americans before 1800, no matter how potentially beneficial, can be suggested for adoption; the opportunity for fundamental political and juridical thought in the U.S. came to an end with the close of the Founding era, rather as divine revelation is thought by Christians to have ceased at the close of the Apostolic Age.

While an intellectual tariff prevents the import of institutional improvements from abroad, Americans are free to export our superior system to the rest of the world. Indeed, doing so is something of a patriotic duty. Otherwise-educated Americans who happen to be completely unaware that our legal tradition is an eccentric deviation from the main tradition of Western jurisprudence do not hesitate to evangelize on behalf of the American Way in matters like criminal justice. In the first few years after the revolutions of 1989 in Europe, when post-communist states in Eastern Europe and Eurasia were debating different models of democratic constitutionalism (and usually concluding that the West German model is preferable to ours), a great number of representatives of the American bar flew into Eastern Europe to sing the praises of our malfunctioning separation-of-powers system and our even more disastrous jury system. My God, I remember thinking at the time, haven't the Eastern Europeans suffered enough?

Dangerous to Democracy

We put up with an electoral system and a constitution in wigs and buckled shoes; why not tolerate a criminal justice system that wears a horned helmet and a bear skin? Here's why we should be concerned: the defects of our particular inherited structures of democratic and constitutional government may be mistakenly interpreted by an alienated public as failures of democracy and constitutionalism as such. The result of such unwarranted but understandable pessimism might be support for plebiscitary rule in politics and, perhaps, vigilantism in law enforcement. Huey Long [Louisiana governor and senator of the early twentieth century] will clean out the crooked statehouse; [action movie stars] Charles Bronson or Clint Eastwood will punish the murderers who get off on technicalities. Legality cannot exist for long in the absence of legitimacy. In a contest between a law that seems to regularly produce unjust outcomes and extra-legal justice, rough justice in some form will sooner or later prevail. (How many people have you heard say, in response to news of Simpson's acquittal, "Maybe somebody will give him what he deserves?")

To make the American system of criminal justice work will require intelligent reform, which in turn requires honest criticism and debate. Unfortunately, ever since Pearl Harbor, debate about fundamental institutional reform in this country has been deterred by the implication that critics of American political and legal institutions are traitors, with either "brown" or "red" sympathies. It is worth recalling that from the Civil War to Pearl Harbor we Americans progressed by junking large parts of the obsolete Anglo-American Colonial heritage and eclectically importing institutional innovations from abroad: the research university, the polytechnic and the kindergarten from Germany, the secret ballot from Australia, workmen's compensation from New Zealand, the public museum from France. As Japan has done recently, we shamelessly copied other nations and frequently improved on what we copied. During that era of American flexibility and progress, Oliver Wendell Holmes Jr., nobody's idea of a flaming radical, observed in connection with the common-law tradition that the mere fact that a statute goes back to the time of Henry VIII is not an argument in its favor.

In the spirit of the enlightened conservatism of Justice Holmes, we need to audit our inherited institutions, rescuing what is vital by carving away the deadwood. We can begin by admitting that some of the foreigners who look aghast at spectacles like the Simpson trial actually may have something to teach us about devising a criminal justice system capable of telling right from wrong.

The Criminal Jury System Is the Best Means to Secure Justice

Barbara Allen Babcock

The 1995 O.J. Simpson verdict, in which the former football star was acquitted of murder, led to numerous calls for jury reform, or even elimination of the criminal jury system. In response, Barbara Allen Babcock, a law professor at Stanford University and the former director of the Public Defender Service in Washington, D.C., wrote a defense of juries and the adversarial system of American justice. Acknowledging that juries do occasionally acquit a guilty defendant based on prejudice or misguided community standards, she notes that conviction rates have been quite consistent for fifty years. Drawing on her own experience as a public defender, she commends juries for their fairness and wisdom, even in cases that she lost. In addition, she takes on certain proposed reforms, explaining that unanimous verdicts and peremptory challenges, which are under attack, are integral parts of the jury system. For Babcock, reforms could actually make juries more unpredictable and less fair. Finally, she suggests that the real problems lie elsewhere, in overworked and unprepared defense counsels and in the vast discrepancy between the rich and the poor when it comes to defending themselves in court.

Barbara Allen Babcock, "In Defense of the Criminal Jury," *Postmortem: The O.J. Simpson Case,* edited by Jeffrey Abramson. New York: BasicBooks, 1996. Copyright © 1996 by BasicBooks. Reproduced by permission of HarperCollins Publishers, Inc.

I personally would have a reasonable doubt, but it's true there is overwhelming evidence that he is possibly guilty.

African-American man interviewed on TV
shortly before the verdict in People v. Simpson

These words reveal the tension in our jury system: "Overwhelming evidence" may lead only to the "possibility" of guilt; in its face, the jury may still entertain a reasonable doubt.

Even without a reasonable doubt, a jury may decide that a defendant deserves freedom. This is the doctrine of nullification—an unspoken possibility in every case. The law itself is nullified, not for all time but as it applies to a single individual. A father who steals to feed his children is the classic example.

In modern times, protestors against government policy, accused of destroying property or of trespassing, have asked the jury to nullify in order to make a political statement. Some have suggested that the mostly African-American jury in the Simpson case was nullifying the law in order to send a message about the racism of the police, and the alienation of black America.

Juries Do Make Mistakes

Without nullifying, juries may simply make mistakes, may be swayed by passion, prejudice, or sympathy to acquit a guilty person, may misread the evidence, or misconstrue their duty. The first Simpson jurors to speak out seemed to say that they took quite literally the judge's instruction that they might discount altogether the evidence of anybody who lied to them in some respects. Thus, disbelieving the police who swore they failed to obtain a search warrant because Simpson was not a suspect, or who made a sweeping denial about using racial epithets, the jury may have mistrusted everything else these officers said. In effect, the lay people may have enforced the exclusionary rules that many judges no longer follow.

Another reading of the Simpson verdict is that the jurors misunderstood reasonable doubt and demanded that every piece of evidence meet that standard. Correctly applied, reasonable doubt requires only that, looking at the case as a whole, its central elements must be proved to the ultimate level.

Even as individual jurors come forward, however, and as books on the trial accumulate, we will not fully understand the dynamics that led to acquittal in this case. In the ancient parlance, the verdict is "inscrutable." Like the ballot, it is the people's announcement of a result, not a set of findings of fact and conclusions of law such as we ideally require from judges when they decide cases.

Losing Faith in Juries Would Be a Bigger Mistake

While acknowledging its inscrutability, many people (I am one) believe that the Simpson verdict was not true or accurate. Yet it would be a mistake to turn our frustration and anger upon the criminal jury itself. Far worse than letting a guilty man go would be losing faith in, or working fundamental changes on, this most American of institutions.

Before the Simpson verdict was in, partly in response to other notorious cases involving unpopular jury results (the acquittal in the first Rodney King beating case, the hung jury in the Menendez parricide), legislative moves were afoot to abolish the unanimity requirement, to reduce the number of jurors, and to eliminate the peremptory challenge. The basic problem with theses proposals is twofold: they wrongly assume that the jury system is broken; they could profoundly change its operation in unpredictable ways.

Conviction Rates Are Consistently High Despite Notorious Acquittals

Behind the bold proposals for jury reform is the bald desire for more convictions. Yet proponents of change do not recite the current conviction rates, which have remained constant—in the 60 to 70 percent range—over the last fifty years. These are the conviction rates in jury trials—most cases (as high as 90 percent in many places) end in conviction on a guilty plea.

Always attending these high conviction rates have been startling acquittals in a few spectacular cases, defined by the horror of the crime, the celebrity of the accused, or a combination of both, as in the Simpson case. Sometimes the lawyers are famous too and almost always, those who win in the face of overwhelming evidence have money to pay for the best defense.

At the turn of the nineteenth century, Lizzie Borden of Fall River, Massachusetts, was accused of killing her parents with an axe. Her case had these now familiar ingredients: powerful circumstantial evidence, first-rate defense lawyers, press from all over the world, a sequestered (though all-male) jury, who acquitted after twenty minutes of deliberation. No one wanted to believe that a woman of good family would be capable of such brutality. Her lawyer might have been taxed with playing the "lady" card.

Another example, this one from California more than a hundred years ago is the case of Issach Kalloch, who shot an unarmed man in full view of his fellow workers, and of people on the street who saw the killing framed in a large window. His victim was the editor of the *San Francisco Chronicle*. A jury acquitted Kalloch on a sort of justification/temporary insanity theory because the paper had printed scurrilous stories about his father.

These are but two of the historical instances of notorious mistaken verdicts, or verdicts that express community sentiment that is, at best, extra-legal. We have always, from the foundation of the Republic, been willing to sustain the risk that the jury will be wrong. Nothing in the Simpson verdict should change that. For every jury that goes awry, there are a hundred that do the right thing. Lawyers on both sides of the criminal system, former jurors, and most academics who have studied juries, attest to this fact. While the Simpson case was in its long progress, for instance, a South Carolina jury convened for several weeks and returned a verdict of life imprisonment rather than death for a young woman who killed her two little children. It was fitting that a jury should decide this case because no judge has the same power to speak with the voice of the people—to forgive and to redeem.

Faith in Juries Comes from Personal Experience

I myself believe in juries based on my experience as a young lawyer when I tried many cases, losing some and winning others, representing mostly African-American men before mostly African-American juries in the District of Columbia. Though losing a verdict is one of life's crushing blows, I felt in virtually all the cases I saw close up that the jury made a correct, and wise, decision. More than occasionally, I found that jurors who started with one predisposition changed their minds through the deliberative process.

My trials did not make the papers, nor were there cameras in the courtroom. Nor was any jury in my experience so mistreated as the Simpson jury—indeed I suspect that the mismanagement of the jury helped to produce the acquittal. This brings me to the second point about why this case should not occasion sweeping changes in the jury system: the point of unintended consequences. We do not know what makes juries work well most of the time, which of its features are necessary to its proper functioning.

The jury comes to us with certain historical attributes: the mystical number twelve; the absolute power to acquit without accountability; the judicial filtering of the evidence heard; the requirement that jurors come from the geographical community where the crime occurred; and that they engage each other to the point of total agreement. No one knows which, if any, of these attributes is essential to the integrity of the institution.

Judge's Mistakes in the Simpson Trial

We do know, however, that a jury should be assembled once for a single purpose, that it should be composed of strangers who know each other only through their deliberations. This fundamental feature of a jury was violated in the Simpson case by a starstruck judge who lost control of the situation. He caused the jury to spend many hours waiting while he heard and reheard lawyers' arguments, took time off to engage celebrities, and through it all, patronized the jurors, conveying by his tone and manner that their time was not important. He should have taken drastic measures to move the trial along, for instance, by hearing motions in the evenings or holding court on Saturdays. Instead, by his leisurely approach, he violated the very premises of the jury system and opened up the possibility that this jury would become a little band with its own agenda.

Judge Ito, like most judges, was largely on his own in deciding how to deal with this jury. In virtually all jurisdictions, the statutes and common law on the selection, care, and instruction of juries are a hodgepodge of rules adopted piecemeal, often in reaction to unpopular verdicts, without concern for how the system as a whole will be affected. A recent voter's initiative in California, for instance, removed the right of lawyers to question potential jurors. By the report of both prosecutors and defenders this law hampers efforts to identify and remove erratic, unstable jurors who can prevent effective deliberation, and may even cause the jury to hang.

The opportunity for lawyers to question prospective jurors (and to follow up troubling answers with more questions) may help select jurors who can return unanimous verdicts. In a similar role, the peremptory challenge allows each side to eliminate the extremes against its position, leaving jurors with middling attitudes who can reach consensus. Yet a move is on, which I will discuss, to abolish these challenges. This is another instance in which reformers neglect the central point that the jury is a collection of interconnected practices and conventions.

Another of the piecemeal jury "reforms" urged in the wake of the Simpson case and other recent unpopular verdicts is to allow nonunanimous jury decisions. As it turned out, of course, the Simpson case is not particularly apt as an example for the reformers, because the jury was unanimous for acquittal. Even had it hung along racial lines, as many pundits predicted it would, the result of permitting nonunanimous verdicts would still have been to acquit Simpson.

Advantages of Unanimous Verdicts

But those who are seizing this moment—in which a famous athlete may get away with murder—to push for majority verdicts risk changing the very nature of the institution. First and most important, a group that must bring along those who see the world differently is more likely to deliberate and discuss the evidence thoroughly. This point is crucial because we have entered a period in which white women and minorities are finally being summoned to jury service in new numbers. In some places, our juries are as diverse as our communities. This is the wrong time to provide for simply outvoting the newcomers. In other words, if there are two or three minority members on a jury of twelve, a system that required that they be convinced to join the verdict, which is our system, seems far better than one in which they serve only to be outvoted.

Finally, a unanimous verdict is a major accomplishment, and carries with it moral authority that a split decision lacks. This point is easily understood when we talk about multi-judge appellate courts, and applies even more forcefully to a judgment from the people. Of course, the Simpson verdict shows that unanimity does not guarantee popularity or credibility, yet surely a 10-2 result with the jury divided along racial lines would have been worse.

My devotion to the unanimity requirement began many years ago when one juror in a case I defended held out for three days against the other eleven and finally convinced them to return a not guilty verdict. Oddly enough, this was the only time in which I put the first twelve people in the box, i.e., I did not use any of my peremptory challenges.

Importance of Peremptory Challenges

That experience does not, however, lead me to think that we should abolish peremptory challenges—another current suggestion for "fixing" the jury. The move has gathered currency because the use of the challenge to strike off white women and minorities has led the Supreme Court to create a sort of modified peremptory. Neither side may challenge a juror on the basis of race or gender. In effect, the Court has created a juror's right to serve. The difficulties of administering jury selection with this modified peremptory challenge as well as the time it can take has roused a call to abolish peremptories altogether.

To reiterate, the parts of the jury fit together, and lopping off one part may cripple it in unforeseeable ways. The function of the parties in striking off biased extremes is interconnected with the unanimity requirement. A second reason for preserving the peremptory is its importance to defendants: they should not face juries that contain people they fear or hate, even for irrational reasons. This is especially true now when long prison sentences are the norm.

Rather than reactive legislation undermining unanimity or the peremptory challenge, a comprehensive statute that preserves the jury's fundamental attributes would be a good outcome of the Simpson verdict. Such a statute should include, for example, provisions regularizing selection practices, including a requirement of juror questionnaires tailored to the facts of the individual case, provision for expedited procedures in cases of sequestration, and for more reasonable compensation and treatment of jurors than we have now. It might also reduce the number of peremptories on both sides, or even eliminate them altogether for the prosecutor, who with a broad general interest in justice should be willing to abide the verdict of the people.

Inadequate Defense Is the Problem, Not Juries

While improvements such as these would be welcome, the mechanics of juries are not at the fault line of the criminal justice system. Especially in the cases that most need community understanding—where defendants are poor people, often racial minorities, charged with horrendous crimes—most juries never have a fair shot at deciding because the defense lawyer is inadequate. When this is the case, the arguments about unanimity, and its connection with peremptory challenges, and whether peremptory challenges are necessary, are all beside the point. Many years ago, Supreme Court Justice Hugo Black wrote that there can be no equal justice when the kind of trial a man gets depends on the amount of money he has. But Black's admonition still only states a hope.

When we think about the Simpson case, we should consider as well *People v. Mayfield*, tried a few years ago in another Los Angeles court. The state's highest court upheld the conviction. Like Orenthal J. Simpson, Demetrie L. Mayfield was a black defendant accused of killing a woman he knew well and a man who appears to have been in the wrong place at the wrong time.

That is about where the similarity ends. Simpson had a team of a dozen lawyers plus forensic pathologists, criminal investigators, and an army of paralegals to defend him. When reporters asked the price tag for all these people, the knowledgeable answer was another question: "How much does he have?" Whatever the final dollar amount, perhaps discounted for the free on-camera advertising, the verdict shows the results of hundreds of hours in preparation and translates into millions of dollars.

Mayfield's attorney, by contrast, practiced alone. According to court records, his entire preparation for the case took forty hours. The attorney conducted only one substantive interview with his client—on the morning the trial began.

Lawyers who appealed Mayfield's conviction argued, as is common in capital cases, that the low level of representation violated his right under the Constitution's Sixth Amendment to the "effective assistance of counsel." Because a series of Supreme Court decisions has lowered the standard for what effective assistance means, those claims are increasingly difficult to make. In Mayfield's case, appellate judges conceded that the defense was less than zealous but concluded that no harm had been done. The evidence was so overwhelming that no defense would have helped much anyway, the courts ruled. Mayfield now sits on Death Row.[1]

Too Often, the Deck Is Stacked Against Defendants

His case is not necessarily the most disturbing—no obvious lawyer errors mar the record. There are many worse cases, some in which appellate courts are forced even to overturn convictions. Indeed, our entire system, with its understaffed prosecutors, overcrowded court dockets and harried public

1. On November 7, 2001, the Ninth Circuit Court of Appeals struck down Demetrie Mayfield's death sentence, based on inadequate representation.

defenders, survives only because of a seldom acknowledged bargain: we provide extensive rights to criminal defendants in theory, but do so in a system that allows mostly the affluent to employ those rights in practice.

If every accused defended himself as Simpson did, the criminal justice system would rapidly collapse. I am not suggesting that every defendant should be provided the resources to press as far as Simpson did. But there is, or should be, something in between the rich man's defense and hardly any defense at all.

When the Simpson case started, I thought that it would provide a popular primer on our American criminal justice system. But as it turned out, the case was no good as a prototype, nor does where it went wrong tell us anything about the changes we should make. It would only compound the errors if this freakish episode led us to transform the way that juries operate.

The criminal jury, right or wrong, is still one of our most precious and characteristically American institutions. Like universal suffrage, with its vote for every citizen regardless of class, race, or gender, the interposition of a jury drawn from the community between the accused and the state is fundamental to our kind of democracy.

The Origins of the American Bill of Rights

The U.S. Constitution as it was originally created and submitted to the colonies for ratification in 1787 did not include what we now call the Bill of Rights. This omission was the cause of much controversy as Americans debated whether to accept the new Constitution and the new federal government it created. One of the main concerns voiced by opponents of the document was that it lacked a detailed listing of guarantees of certain fundamental individual rights. These critics did not succeed in preventing the Constitution's ratification, but were in large part responsible for the existence of the Bill of Rights.

In 1787 the United States consisted of thirteen former British colonies that had been loosely bound since 1781 by the Articles of Confederation. Since declaring their independence from Great Britain in 1776, the former colonies had established their own colonial governments and constitutions, eight of which had bills of rights written into them. One of the most influential was Virginia's Declaration of Rights. Drafted largely by planter and legislator George Mason in 1776, the seventeen-point document combined philosophical declarations of natural rights with specific limitations on the powers of government. It served as a model for other state constitutions.

The sources for these declarations of rights included English law traditions dating back to the 1215 Magna Carta and the 1689 English Bill of Rights—two historic documents that provided specific legal guarantees of the "true, ancient, and indubitable rights and liberties of the people" of England. Other legal sources included the colonies' original charters, which declared that colonists should have the same "privileges, franchises, and immunities" that they would if they lived in England. The ideas concerning natural rights developed by John Locke and other English philosophers were also influential. Some of these concepts of rights had been cited in the Declaration of Independence to justify the American Revolution.

Unlike the state constitutions, the Articles of Confederation, which served as the national constitution from 1781 to 1788, lacked a bill of rights. Because the national government under the Articles of Confederation had little authority by design, most people believed it posed little threat to civil liberties, rendering a bill of rights unnecessary. However, many influential leaders criticized the very weakness of the national government for creating its own problems; it did not create an effective system for conducting a coherent foreign policy, settling disputes between states, printing money, and coping with internal unrest.

It was against this backdrop that American political leaders convened in Philadelphia in May 1787 with the stated intent to amend the Articles of Confederation. Four months later the Philadelphia Convention, going beyond its original mandate, created a whole new Constitution with a stronger national government. But while the new Constitution included a few provisions protecting certain civil liberties, it did not include any language similar to Virginia's Declaration of Rights. Mason, one of the delegates in Philadelphia, refused to sign the document. He listed his objections in an essay that began:

> There is no Declaration of Rights, and the Laws of the general government being paramount to the laws and constitution of the several States, the Declaration of Rights in the separate States are no security.

Mason's essay was one of hundreds of pamphlets and other writings produced as the colonists debated whether to ratify the new Constitution (nine of the thirteen colonies had to officially ratify the Constitution for it to go into effect). The supporters of the newly drafted Constitution became known as Federalists, while the loosely organized group of opponents were called Antifederalists. Antifederalists opposed the new Constitution for several reasons. They believed the presidency would create a monarchy, Congress would not be truly representative of the people, and state governments would be endangered. However, the argument that proved most effective was that the new document lacked a bill of rights and thereby threatened Americans with the loss of cherished individual liberties. Federalists realized that to gain the support of key states such as New York and Virginia, they needed to pledge to offer amendments to the Constitution that would be added immediately after its ratification. Indeed, it was not until this promise was made that the requisite number of colonies ratified the document. Massachusetts, Virginia, South Carolina, New Hampshire, and New York all included amendment recommendations as part of their decisions to ratify.

One of the leading Federalists, James Madison of Virginia, who was elected to the first Congress to convene under the new Constitution, took the lead in drafting the promised amendments. Under the process provided for in the Constitution, amendments needed to be passed by both the Senate and House of Representatives and then ratified by three-fourths of the states. Madison sifted through the suggestions provided by the states and drew upon the Virginia Declaration of Rights and other state documents in composing twelve amendments, which he introduced to Congress in September 1789. "If they are incorporated into the constitution," he argued in a speech introducing his proposed amendments,

Independent tribunals of justice will consider themselves in a peculiar manner the guardians of those rights; they will be an impenetrable bulwark against every assumption of power in the legislative or executive; they will be naturally led to resist every encroachment upon rights expressly stipulated for in the constitution by the declaration of rights.

After debate and some changes to Madison's original proposals, Congress approved the twelve amendments and sent them to the states for ratification. Two amendments were not ratified; the remaining ten became known as the Bill of Rights. Their ratification by the states was completed on December 15, 1791.

Supreme Court Cases Involving
the Right to a Trial by Jury

1794

Georgia v. Brailsford

The jury has the power to judge the law in bringing a verdict.

1866

Ex Parte Milligan

Military tribunals may not try civilians.

1874

Edwards v. Elliott

Trial by jury is a guaranteed right in civil cases before federal courts, but not necessarily before state courts. (State courts still have considerably more flexibility in civil cases than they do in criminal cases.)

1888

Callan v. Wilson

Trial by jury cannot be involuntarily set aside for offenses "of a grave nature" (though for "petty or minor offenses," it may be denied).

1895

Sparf v. United States

Juries do not have to be informed of their power to judge the law, as well as the facts.

1898

Thompson v. State of Utah

Federal juries in criminal cases must conform to English common law, which requires a twelve-person, unanimous verdict.

1930

Patton v. United States
Defendants have the right to waive trial by jury. In this case, Patton was convicted by an eleven-person jury after agreeing to dismissal of the twelfth juror. He later argued that he actually could not agree to dismissing the juror, since doing so denied him trial by a true jury. The Court agreed in part, arguing that eleven was insufficient for a jury, but found that his agreement constituted a waiver of his right to jury trial. Subsequent rulings have modified this twelve-member requirement.

1948

Frazier v. United States
In the absence of proof of bias, the fact that jurors all come from a particular category (in this case, government employees in a District of Columbia jury) does not automatically violate the right to an impartial jury.

1963

Kennedy v. Mendoza-Martinez
Denationalization, or the stripping of one's citizenship, constitutes a punitive action that mandates Fifth and Sixth Amendment protections, including the right to trial by jury.

1965

Turner v. Louisiana
Fraternization between prosecution witnesses (in this case, state sheriffs) and juries may constitute a violation of jury impartiality.

1968

Duncan v. Louisiana
The right to trial by jury is a fundamental (Fourteenth Amendment) right that extends to state courts and, unless waived, must be allowed in trying "serious crimes."

Witherspoon v. Illinois
While it is permissible in capital cases to exclude jurors who absolutely will not impose the death penalty (so-called Witherspoon excludables), it is not permissible to dismiss all jurors who simply oppose the death penalty philosophically.

1970

Baldwin v. New York
A crime with a punishment of possible imprisonment of more than six months should be considered a "serious" crime and requires a jury trial, unless defendant waives this right.

Williams v. Florida
The twelve-person jury is not a strict requirement, and a smaller jury can be equally effective in preventing "oppression by the Government."

1972

Apodaca v. Oregon
This decision essentially confirmed the decision in *Johnson v. Louisiana*, finding that a majority verdict did not effectively exclude minority jurors.

Johnson v. Louisiana
Less than unanimous jury decisions are permissible in certain cases.

1973

Colgrove v. Battin
As in *Williams v. Florida*, the Court held that a six-person jury is sufficient, this time in civil cases.

1975

Taylor v. Louisiana
Women cannot be excluded from potential jury service or given automatic exemptions.

1977

Castaneda v. Partida
A pattern of underrepresentation of a particular class or ethnic group in juries (in this case, the grand jury) constitutes discrimination and thus violates the right to trial by an impartial, representative jury.

1978

Ballew v. Georgia
Five-person juries are too small for "nonpetty" offenses.

1979

Burch v. Louisiana
Six-person juries must deliver unanimous verdicts. A five-to-one decision is not sufficient.

1986

Batson v. Kentucky
Prosecutors cannot use peremptory challenges to exclude all jurors of a particular race.

Lockhart v. McCree
While the jury panel (venire) from which jurors are drawn must represent a cross-section of the community, juries themselves do not have to be representative of this cross-section.

2000

Apprendi v. New Jersey
Prosecutors must submit any fact that increases the penalty for a crime beyond the maximum sentence (except for prior convictions) to a jury for deliberation.

2002

Ring v. Arizona
Any aggravating circumstances that would lead to a death sentence must be heard and deliberated by a jury. Otherwise, the judge cannot impose the death penalty.

Books

Jeffrey Abramson, *We, the Jury: The Jury System and the Ideal of Democracy*. New York: BasicBooks, 1994.

James Alexander, *A Brief Narrative of the Case and Trial of John Peter Zenger*. Ed. Stanley Nider Katz. Cambridge, MA: Belknap, 1972.

Bernard Bailyn, ed., *The Debate on the Constitution*. New York: Library of America, 1993.

John Baldwin and Michael McConville, *Jury Trials*. Oxford, UK: Clarendon Press, 1979.

William Blackstone, *Commentaries on the Laws of England*. Oxford, UK: Clarendon Press, 1769.

Clay S. Conrad, *Jury Nullification: The Evolution of a Doctrine*. Durham, NC: Carolina Academic Press, 1998.

Paula DiPerna, *Juries on Trial: Faces of American Justice*. New York: Dembner, 1984.

William Forsyth, *History of Trial by Jury*. Jersey City, NJ: Frederick D. Linn, 1875.

Jeffrey T. Frederick, *The Psychology of the American Jury*. Charlottesville, VA: Michie, 1987.

Thomas Andrew Green, *Verdict According to Conscience: Perspectives on the English Criminal Trial Jury, 1200–1800*. Chicago: University of Chicago Press, 1985.

Francis H. Heller, *The Sixth Amendment to the Constitution of the United States: A Study in Constitutional Development*. Lawrence: University of Kansas Press, 1951.

Randolph N. Jonakait, *The American Jury System*. New Haven, CT: Yale University Press, 2003.

Harry Kalven Jr. and Hans Zeisel, *The American Jury*. Chicago: University of Chicago Press, 1970.

Godfrey D. Lehman, *We the Jury: The Impact of Jurors on Our Basic Freedoms: Great Jury Trials of History*. Amherst, NY: Prometheus, 1997.

James P. Levine, *Juries and Politics*. Pacific Grove, CA: Brooks/Cole, 1992.

Leonard W. Levy, *The Palladium of Justice: Origins of Trial by Jury*. Chicago: Ivan R. Dee, 1999.

Robert E. Litan, ed., *Verdict: Assessing the Civil Jury System*. Washington, DC: Brookings Institution, 1993.

William Nelson, *Americanization of the Common Law: The Impact of Legal Change in Massachusetts Society, 1760–1830*. Cambridge, MA: Harvard University Press, 1975.

Gregory D. Russell, *The Death Penalty and Racial Bias: Overturning Supreme Court Assumptions*. Westport, CT: Greenwood, 1994.

Robert Scigliano, ed., *The Federalist: A Commentary on the Constitution of the United States*. New York: Modern Library, 2001.

Lysander Spooner, *An Essay on the Trial by Jury*. Boston: John P. Jewett, 1852.

Shannon Stimson, *The American Revolution in the Law: Anglo-American Jurisprudence Before John Marshall*. Princeton, NJ: Princeton University Press, 1990.

Joseph Story, *Commentaries on the Constitution of the United States*. Vol. 2. Reprint, New York: Williams S. Hein, 1994.

Alexis de Tocqueville, *Democracy in America*. Trans. and Ed. Harvey Mansfield and Delba Winthrop. Chicago: University of Chicago Press, 2000.

Web Sites

American Bar Association: FAQ on Grand Juries, www.abanet.org/media/faqjury.html. The American Bar Association, the professional organization for American lawyers, here provides basic answers to questions about the functions and history of the grand jury.

Constitutional Rights Foundation, Chicago: The American Jury, Bulwark of Democracy, www.crfc.org/americanjury. The nonpartisan CRFC is devoted to bringing law-related resources into the classroom. Here it provides background information on the history and development of trial by jury and links for further information and lesson plans.

FindLaw Constitution Center, www.findlaw.com/casecode/ constitution. A clearinghouse site for lawyers, law students, and the general public, this Web site provides links to the text, case law, and judicial interpretation of all the amendments, including the Sixth and Seventh, which cover the right to jury trials.

Fully Informed Jury Association, www.fija.org. From an organization devoted to the concept of jury nullification, this Web site provides numerous background materials on the use of this doctrine throughout American history and guides for prospective jurors.

Judicial Council of California: Jury Project, www.courtinfo. ca.gov/jury. This site, maintained by the California state courts, provides basic information on jury service and trial process for all potential jurors. Most of it is applicable throughout the United States.